A CRY FOR
JUSTICE

SHELLEY **HUNDLEY**

D1115776

CHARISMA
HOUSE

Most CHARISMA HOUSE BOOK GROUP products are available at special quantity discounts for bulk purchase for sales promotions, premiums, fund-raising, and educational needs. For details, write Charisma House Book Group, 600 Rinehart Road, Lake Mary, Florida 32746, or telephone (407) 333-0600.

A CRY FOR JUSTICE by Shelley E. Hundley
Published by Charisma House
Charisma Media/Charisma House Book Group
600 Rinehart Road
Lake Mary, Florida 32746
www.charismahouse.com

Cover design by Justin Evans
Design Director: Bill Johnson

Visit the author's website at www.ihop.org.

Library of Congress Cataloging-in-Publication Data:

Hundley, Shelley E.
    A cry for justice / Shelley E. Hundley. -- 1st ed.
        p. cm.
    Includes bibliographical references (p.   ).
    ISBN 978-1-61638-259-9 (trade paper) -- ISBN 978-1-61638-571-2 (e-book) 1. Hundley, Shelley E. 2. Christian converts--Biography. 3. Conversion--Christianity--Biography. 4. Suffering--Religious aspects--Christianity. 5. Healing--Religious aspects--Christianity. I. Title.
    BV4935.H795A3 2011
    248.2'46092--dc23
    [B]

                                        2011022391

First Edition

11 12 13 14 15 — 987654321
Printed in the United States of America

AUTHOR'S NOTE: Some names, places, and identifying details with regard to stories in this book have been changed to help protect the privacy of individuals who may have been involved in those experiences.

CONTENTS

FOREWORD

IN A CULTURE permeated with relativism, humanism, and toleration, the church faces the temptation to shy away from the biblical teachings of a God who brings forth righteous judgment to confront oppression and make wrong things right. Yet this is one of the most neglected attributes of Jesus's love for His people. Today the Holy Spirit is revealing the beauty of Jesus in an unprecedented way before His return. We can know Jesus as our Bridegroom who is filled with desire, our King who manifests His power, and our righteous Judge who intervenes to remove all that hinders love.

God's message of comfort includes His commitment to those who suffer. He promises that a day is coming when every wrong thing that is done against us will be made right. Shelley Hundley has addressed this important but difficult subject with biblical clarity and pastoral tenderness. Her vulnerability and courage in sharing her own dramatic and heart-wrenching story will serve many who are seeking a way to find healing for their hearts after being oppressed.

I have seen the impact of Shelley's messages. Thousands have wept with newfound liberty when they understood their dignity and were empowered to walk in holiness and forgiveness toward those who hurt them.

I am grateful for Shelley's excellent ministry and

perseverance. She labored with me and others to start the International House of Prayer on May 7, 1999. Today she is one of the senior leaders over the International House of Prayer University, which has more than a thousand full-time students and interns.

I have witnessed her exemplary life within our community and her sound Bible teaching for more than a decade. I can say without any reservation that Shelley seeks to love Jesus with all of her heart and searches God's Word with great diligence, trembling before it. She serves tirelessly to see others receive the breakthroughs she herself has received from God.

What you hold in your hands is one of the timeliest messages available in this hour. I enthusiastically recommend that you prayerfully read through this book and take its truths into your own personal dialogue with Jesus. Ask the Holy Spirit to reveal to you your need to know the face of Jesus the Judge who answers every cry for justice as He causes us to abound in love for Him and others.

—MIKE BICKLE
FOUNDER, INTERNATIONAL HOUSE OF PRAYER
KANSAS CITY, MISSOURI

INTRODUCTION

I T IS WITH great joy that I invite you to enter the journey of an atheist who turned to God. He has healed my heart with His matchless love and answered my cry for justice. During my painful journey through utter hopelessness, paralyzing depression, and even attempted suicide, I came to know Jesus as the Judge who fights for us. He takes an account of every wrong done and will make all things right.

Knowing Jesus as the Judge who does not grow weary in bringing forth justice has been the greatest comfort of my life. I have come to know without a shadow of a doubt that He sees, He hears, and He knows the depth of our suffering. I believe God wants us all to experience the same comfort. Looking forward to being comforted by the coming Judge was central to the apostle Paul's message to the persecuted church in Thessalonica. (See 1 Thessalonians 4:13–18.) But today, in our relativistic and humanistic culture, this aspect of God's character makes many Christians uncomfortable, so we often shove historic Christian theology on judgment into a corner and no longer mention it in our witness or experience of the gospel.

We treat God's Word on judgment like the drunken uncle we'd like to hide in a back room during family reunions so his behavior doesn't embarrass us. Yet our faith and witness are bankrupt without a true, living knowledge of God as the righteous Judge. Without recognizing Him as our Judge, we have no response to the darkness and torment we see in the earth. We end up no better off than our unbelieving neighbors, withering under the weight of the wickedness and perversion in the world with no answers. We watch the news without hope, seeing no end to the tragedy and no understanding of how the Lord will respond to this evil.

The result is that we simply retreat from our witness of Jesus as we cower under the age-old question of why there is suffering and injustice in the world. Intimidated, we become easily persuaded to avoid any mention of judgment in our evangelism. We say our actions speak louder than words, but the reality is that we are too afraid to speak at all.

We live among people who are hurting, and the church has the answer they are looking for. They need to know that Jesus is the Judge who saw and heard what no one else did and that He will avenge the wrong. Through the heart of Jesus, the Bridegroom Judge, we can come to understand a God who says what happened to us was significant and that someone must pay. Yet in His mercy Jesus offers Himself as the solution and the recipient of the just punishment.

Understanding Jesus as our Judge allows us to truly comprehend forgiveness. We realize that forgiveness is not about Jesus looking the other way but about us entrusting our case to Him. By forgiving what seems impossible to release, we can make the mercy of Jesus famous and plead with those who do not know Christ to call upon Him and receive the forgiveness we have received ourselves.

When we think the wrongs done to us don't matter to God,

we cannot recognize our true worth. Our hearts were made to cry out, "Who will fight for us?" No matter how hard we try to bury that cry, it will fester like a wound unless we come to know Jesus the Judge. As someone who has experienced the pain of abuse, I know how hard it is to express the anguish that comes when your innocence is violently stolen in an instant, when your mouth is muffled and your soul is silenced. I don't think human language is supposed to adequately describe these things hell has invented.

Yet somehow, even in these places, God shows Himself mighty. In my darkest pain and my darkest moments, there was a Judge. He came with a strong hand. He came with vengeance in His eyes, and with just one look from His fiery gaze I knew I was worth so much to Him. Now I can forget the horror of what happened because He never will.

Will you join me in allowing Jesus, the Bridegroom Judge, to take us into His counsel? It is my prayer that He will ignite in our hearts the fire of His love and the fear of the Lord so that in this great hour of shaking we might understand His heart and turn back to God. This book was written for one reason. You need a Judge!

Chapter One

WHY I BECAME AN ATHEIST

WHEN I ENTERED college at the age of seventeen, I was an avowed atheist, and I quickly distinguished myself on campus as one of the most hostile and defiant people to the message of Jesus. This was no small thing because I attended a Christian college where the gospel was preached often, including at mandatory chapel services.

I wasn't always this way. The daughter of American missionaries, I was born in Medellín, Colombia, and reared on the campus of a seminary that trained leaders to serve in what was one of the most violent nations in the world.

Murder and kidnapping were commonplace, and it was hardly unusual for my family to hear bomb blasts and gun fights on our street. In fact, I grew up thinking this was normal. I went to bed each night to the sound of attack dogs unleashed at 10:00 p.m. to prevent thieves or hired assassins from breaking into the seminary and killing or kidnapping one of the many missionary families who lived there. I knew of many believers who lost their lives when guerrillas burst into church services and sprayed bullets in the sanctuary. Even at a young age, I knew what it meant to suffer for Jesus. I saw people do it almost every day.

Although my childhood was anything but easy, I never

resented living in Colombia. I thought Medellín was a beautiful place. It had perpetual springlike weather that made the brilliant landscape seem to be always bursting with life. From my perspective as a child, the Cordillera mountains seemed to wrap themselves around Colombia's second largest city like a warm hug, protecting the fruit trees, wild orchids, and South American wildlife that thrive in its lush valley.

When I was a little girl, I often would slip out to the front porch in the evenings just to take in Medellín's beauty. As sunlight fled and darkness took its watch, the city lights flickered across the sky like a magic show, climbing the sides of the mountains and then spreading out in every direction. The beauty and safety I felt as I looked at the mountains never meshed with the terror, violence, and death that shrouded the city and gripped its inhabitants with fear.

A Climate of Fear

Everyone seemed to have the same nagging yet unspoken question, "How long?" How long will the violence continue? How long until the next person disappears? How long before the guerrillas spill more innocent blood in the streets? No one said this out loud, but no one had to. It was in the eyes of every Colombian and anyone who had lived in the nation long enough to be infected by this contagious feeling of dread. Violence was as constant in Colombia as sunrise and sunset.

With the advent of the drug years in the 1980s, Colombia fell into a downward spiral of political chaos and staggering suffering. A relentless underground cocaine industry and a vicious hierarchy of drug lords backed Marxist guerrillas.

These rebels took over the Palace of Justice, which was the equivalent of the US Pentagon, as frightened Colombians watched the real-life drama unfold on their TV sets.

At the height of its "narco" (narcotics) years, Medellín was ruled by a drug lord named Pablo Escobar. He bred an environment of instability and unpredictability, and unspeakable bloodshed seemed to lurk around every corner. At any moment, a store or a restaurant might be blown up, massacring everyone in the vicinity, just because Pablo wanted to settle a score.

The danger was at such a height that my mom sat me down once before a visit to the dentist and reminded me not to give out any information about our family—what we did, where we lived, how many siblings I had. She told me, "Remember, Shelley, anyone could be a guerrilla, even people who seem nice. Nurses and dentists can be killers or kidnappers." As a little girl, I struggled to understand what all of this meant. I pictured normal people taking off their masks and revealing their true identities as guerrillas, whatever those were. All I knew was that these guerrillas weren't animals; they were men and women, sometimes even children, who had killed people we knew, kidnapping children and adults alike.

The other constant in Colombia was unspeakable poverty. Even as a child, I could never get over the despair and deprivation around me every day. I played soccer with neighborhood kids who had only one pair of shorts to their names and actually picked pockets to secure food and other essentials. This was so well known, the neighborhood children who came into the seminary were frisked on their way out to ensure they didn't steal anything. This always seemed unfair to me at the time, but I understand it was necessary. Once, we missionary kids devised a scheme to turn the tables on the adults. We stole all the seminary professors' wallets; then at the end of the day, when the neighborhood children were being frisked, we returned the wallets, grinning ear to ear.

As you may have guessed, I had an adventurous and sometimes mischievous personality. I caused a little trouble here and there for sneaking too much food to my friends or for refusing to wear new shoes or clothes because my play-mates had none. But I also had fun despite my dangerous surroundings. I loved to play soccer with my big brothers, and I tried to keep up with all of their crazy stunts.

The hills across this paradise were great for sliding, and bamboo groves made the best kids' bows and arrows you could ever wish for. I especially liked to climb the mango trees. I'd carry my pocketknife in one hand and a little bag of lemon and salt in my pocket to dip my fresh mango slices in. Truth be told, I ruined my appetite for dinner many times with my mango eating, and it was a constant source of tension between my mom and me.

Medellín was like the times Charles Dickens described in *A Tale of Two Cities*: full of the best and the worst. It was a constant contradiction—good and bad, happy and sad, beauty and pain, paradise and poverty. I had the honor of being surrounded by missionaries who had left everything to serve the Lord and by radical Colombian believers who were ready to die for Christ. Many received the chance to do so. Some Colombian Christians were assassinated in the very churches where they worshiped because of their opposition to the Marxist guerrillas' call for violent revolution.

Americans too were targeted for murder and kidnapping as retaliation for the arrests of Colombian drug lords who were extradited to the United States to be tried for their crimes. My brothers and I had the equivalent of "snow days" when the US Embassy would call to warn our parents that there were new death threats against Americans, so we couldn't go outside or be near the windows.

Although violence hounded us, I considered Colombia my home. So when my parents decided to move to Indiana just before I entered eighth grade, I felt like the ground beneath me had been removed. My identity was deeply rooted in my cross-cultural experience in Medellín. I was a *gringa-paisa*, an American by blood but a Colombian by birth.

My family had lived in the United States for short periods of time, and the thought of leaving a nation and people I loved to move to a country whose rules I couldn't seem to figure out pierced my twelve-year-old heart. I told my parents I wouldn't leave and threatened to run away from home, but then reality began to sink in. The prospect of running away in a city where I would certainly be kidnapped didn't seem to be a viable option either, so I begrudgingly surrendered to the move.

In Indiana, I trudged through middle and high school, dealing with major culture shock and struggling to make friends, though my gifts in music won me some friendships. Looking back I don't think my experience in high school was much different from other American kids my age.

I visited my church's youth group and attended their retreats. I even longed for intimacy with God at this young age, but I never sensed a breakthrough in my heart. I always felt like I was outside of God's presence, incapable of even looking in. Real intimacy with Jesus always seemed just out of reach.

Buried Memories

In the midst of all my normal teenage challenges, I was grappling with feelings of self-hatred that I just couldn't shake. On many nights I would sit huddled in my bedroom just sobbing in the darkness because I couldn't make the shame and self-loathing go away. Terror would overwhelm me, and images of sexual abuse would flood my mind.

I didn't know how to process these thoughts. I didn't want to believe they represented actual experiences, but something was deeply wrong in my heart. I saw a girl huddled on the floor of an old Spanish-style home in Medellín. She had long wavy hair that seemed to be a mixture of light brown, blonde, and amber. And her soft blue eyes were filled with too much sadness for a child of only eight. Hugging her knees tightly to her chest, she buried her face and cried because someone bigger and stronger had forced himself on her, and I had the sense it wasn't the first time this had happened.

The girl sat there wishing she had never been born and fearing when the abuse might happen again. She sputtered out jumbled phrases amid her tears and heavy breathing, "Why does this keep happening? When will it all stop?" Her breathing got heavier and heavier until she felt as though her lungs were filled with heavy iron. Each second made her feel more and more anchored to the cold tile floor.

When the tears finally stopped, she felt a numb, empty feeling wash over her. She felt this every time she suffered abuse. This man hadn't been the first. He was the third person who had done this to her, but this time had been the worst ever.

Sitting there, cold and limp, she shuddered as she remembered how he had threatened her so she wouldn't tell. But she was past the point of trying to figure out a way to tell someone, to stop the horror from happening again. She felt doomed to serve out a sentence she was beginning to think she must deserve. She thought that surely the torment must have been her fault somehow.

She looked so small and alone there on the floor as she recalled the man's threats. "If you tell people, they will all know how perverse you really are and how you bring this on yourself. Do you want everyone to see what you really are?" His words seemed to burn into her brain, and she couldn't make them go away. "God must hate me so much, but I just don't know why," she told herself. She thought she might explode because the pain was so great. "I can't make it. I can't make it another day!"

Another wave of weeping and heavy breathing poured out of the girl's exhausted little heart. She remembered how disgusted she felt when she heard the man preach at a church service where the congregation responded so wholeheartedly to his message about holiness. Hearing him preach made her feel ill, but she wondered if that was just further proof that she was only receiving what she deserved. "I must be going to hell!" the little girl muttered. "I must be worthless and horrible and perverse."

Somehow I knew the girl had accepted Jesus in Sunday school but couldn't seem to find her Savior amid the confusion, guilt, and despair. "I must be everything he says I am," she told herself. "I must deserve it all." She pounded her body in anger thinking that if her injuries were even more severe, maybe then someone would notice and stop this torture.

Once I saw that she succeeded in getting away. She ran as far as she could, only to realize as she fled that she was in as much or more danger running down the streets of Colombia as she was in the hands of the abuser. Terrified and feeling forlorn, she climbed a tree to the highest branch she could reach and sat there and cried.

No matter where she turned there was nothing but torment. When she was finally able to quiet herself down a little bit, she could hear some of her friends playing outside the house. But she couldn't go out to play. Instead, she sank into a daydream, imagining a day when someone would finally make the pain and abuse stop.

Even when I didn't want to believe that I was this little girl, the images of her and the pain she felt were always there in the background. And no matter what was happening in my mind, I couldn't deny the depression, loneliness, and feelings of worthlessness that plagued my heart even when everything in my teenage life seemed fine.

The images kept coming, and with them an unexplainable repulsion toward one minister our family knew well on the mission field. His face seemed ingrained in all of the images, but still I hoped the scenes of the little girl weren't real. Tormented by these persistent, invasive thoughts, and even more so by the fear that I could never escape them, I retreated even further behind a wall of shame. I did what I could to bury it all.

Facing the Past

I carried these feelings of pain and hopelessness silently for years. Then one month before I left home for college, I had a conversation with someone who had been on the mission field with my family. That meeting changed everything. Completely unaware of the abuse I had suffered, this friend told me that a minister we had known in Colombia was found to have sexually abused children when we were living in Medellín. He listed several children's names, and some of them were my dear friends.

This individual had no idea what was happening in my heart as he told me this. All of a sudden I felt as though I was outside of myself listening to what was being said. I felt cold all over and couldn't control the tremors that came over my body. It seemed as though some dark and tempestuous evil had reached up from the ground and grabbed me by both legs.

The person who spoke with me thought I would be shocked by what was said, but I barely even looked surprised. I knew now without a doubt that all the images that had filled my mind and the pain that kept me up nights crying in terror were real. I kept a cold expression on my face because I wasn't ready to say anything about my own experience. I listened and took in all the information the person offered and asked as many questions as I could without giving away my own story.

When we ended the conversation and I walked away, I began a terrifying journey into the past. In those next moments, I felt as if I was being encircled by hell's fire. I felt fenced in on every side, and I couldn't move. I couldn't talk. The curtain that covered the thing I couldn't name had suddenly been removed, and now I was forced to face the reality of those horrible images. My emotions were all over the place. On one hand I felt a sense of relief as I thought, "I am not the only one. It really was wrong what he did. It wasn't my fault." But on the other hand, a steely, silent sort of rage started rising up in me.

I felt anger that I had never before been able to feel for myself, and it began to rise up as I thought of all the others this man had abused. I was finally beginning to piece together what I had experienced, and I was 100 percent certain that this person had sexually abused me for several years when my family lived in Colombia. The excruciating pain I had locked away deep inside had suddenly been set free and was now moving throughout my being.

I was filled with a quiet but fierce indignation during the silent drive home. I looked out at the road, but all I saw were the events of my life replaying with a new, insidious, hellish fire illuminating the dark, sadistic series of events. This horror wasn't imaginary; it was my real life and the reality of some of my dearest childhood friends. And not only had this man abused me, others had done so as well.

In the car, I felt a heaviness begin to overtake me. Then I had a thought. It seemed like a lofty and wise idea, an indisputable solution to a difficult equation. I felt as though I was rising above my situation and being caught up by a wiser, more definitive conclusion than any I had ever drawn. The evidence had presented itself. It all made sense now. None of what I had heard about Jesus was true. It was all a lie. There is no God. And I should kill myself.

Chapter Two

"DO SOMETHING ABOUT THIS PAIN!"

A T HOME IN Indiana for another month before I left for
college, I felt the terror and trauma of the abuse come
crashing down like an avalanche that needed just one small
rock to fall in order to start its violent descent. The abuse I
had always remembered but never named flooded not just
my mind but also my body. It was as if a faucet long shut off
had been turned on full strength, and fiery poison was now
pouring in, drowning me with gushing force. It is difficult to
describe how it feels to relive something you never thought
you could endure the first time around. The fear and terror
were overwhelming.

Although I was now seventeen years old and no one was
trying to harm me, emotionally I felt like the seven-year-old
who had been slammed onto the floor and abused. I was able
to begin to test the waters a bit by talking with a few individuals I trusted, but I was still unable to get many of the details
out in words. Some of the memories were unbearable to even
think of let alone talk about.

I would be going away to college in Kentucky in about a
month, and one of the few people I had opened up to encouraged me to see a counselor when I arrived at school. With

the little I was able to say at this point, no one else knew the frequency or nature of the sexual and sadistic abuse I silently endured all those years. It was sheer hell on earth. My future counselors would later say my case was one of the most difficult they had ever encountered. Not only had I experienced the pain of abuse, but I also grew up surrounded by death and violence in Colombia.

I was shot at and saw dead bodies along the street on my way to school. One night I opened my bedroom window just as someone was being stabbed in the park in front of my house. I didn't know it at the time, but I was struggling with a severe case of post-traumatic stress disorder. Yet I was doing my best to put on a good face so those around me wouldn't know how strong the suicidal thoughts had become.

I had been looking forward to leaving for college, even if the school wasn't exactly my first choice. In my family, my brothers and I could attend any college we wanted. The catch was that a particular Methodist college was the only one our parents would pay for, at least for the first year. So the Methodist college it was. By the time I arrived on campus, I was a totally different person. Gone was the youth group member, overachiever, talented musician, and caring friend. I was silent, angry, and depressed. I became sarcastic and lashed out at anyone who talked about Jesus or the Bible.

Profanity now filled my speech because I felt I needed a whole new vocabulary to even attempt to express the seething rage and bitterness taking over every part of me. I had two communication modes—silence or a stream of profanity.

There was nothing in between. I had no emotional resource to maintain any pretense.

I felt alone and angry, and it seemed nothing would make those feelings go away. I tried to abuse drugs and alcohol, but for some reason I always got caught right before I actually consumed any of those substances. As I felt the depression taking me over, I reached out for help one last time. During orientation week, before classes even started, I headed up to the counseling office on campus and practically beat the door down.

Someone finally came to the door to let me know the counseling services were not available yet. But after taking a good look at me, she offered me the next available appointment with a counselor. After school started, I went to some counseling sessions, but it all seemed superficial to me, and I couldn't see how any of it would help me. I was dealing with flashbacks, terrifying nightmares, and a weight of depression that made it difficult for me to even walk to my classes, let alone do any of the work.

Meltdown

Everything culminated for me one day when I was attending a counseling group for sexually abused women on my college campus. Until then, I had been accepting all the counseling assistance available on campus. Although I was still fighting thoughts of suicide, I was trying to survive...until this day.

The person leading the group went around the circle asking each of the girls how her week had gone. I had become familiar with these girls who were dealing with pasts similar to mine. I learned early on that there is no scale of pain when it comes to sexual abuse; every inappropriate experience thrown upon a child is devastating to his or her heart, mind, and body.

Each girl in the group shared how her week had gone, and the stories were all the same. One girl said, "Well, I thought about committing suicide constantly, but I didn't actually do it." Another said, "I have been cutting myself a lot all week, but I didn't actually slit my wrist." Still another said, "I was too depressed to get out of bed all week, but at least I didn't have the energy to harm myself." The counselor meant well, but her response was trite. She said something along the lines of, "Each of you is making progress, and you will make it through this difficult time. There is a light at the end of the tunnel."

Her words seemed hollow to my analytical mind that constantly judged and criticized everything I heard. I remember very well the first words that came out of my mouth at the support group that day. I took a breath, looked the counselor squarely in the eye, and slowly and deliberately said, "You…have…nothing." Then the barrage came. I laid it all out: the counselor's inability to identify with any of our experiences of abuse, her detachment from the despair that made up every moment of our existence, and lastly the real fate that awaited all of us.

I remember raising my voice at the counselor and demanding, "At least be honest with us. You don't have any real hope that any of us will undergo any real change. Your greatest hope is that somehow we will talk about what happened to us long enough for it to lose a little bit of its sadistic hold on our lives. And *hopefully*, if we become comfortable enough with the atrocities we have experienced, then *somehow* we at least won't harm others or ourselves."

I pleaded with the counselor, who now had lost all color in her face, "Come on, be honest with us. That's your real hope, isn't it? You can't do anything to take away what any of us have lived through, and we are unwilling to live with the pain and shame of it all! You don't have any real hope that any of us will be happy or normal again. We are all doomed to carry the horror and torment for the rest of our lives. You are powerless to actually change any of it."

I then turned to the girls and began laying out my conclusion. "Only by ending our lives could we end the torment we were facing and avoid hurting others or becoming an unwanted burden upon society. No one else can make us better or do anything to undo one ounce of what has been done to us, so let's end the whole farce now and take the logical step of committing suicide. Surely this is the wisest and most reasonable action we could take for ourselves and for society."

I was calm and matter-of-fact. My appeal wasn't frantic and emotional, and I felt I had made a logical and compelling case. In my mind, it truly was the only way. Looking back, I now see this moment as a demonic preaching episode. My gifts were working against me during this period of my life. Having concluded my speech, I lowered my head and stared at a design on the carpet.

Silently, I was finalizing my own plan for suicide while everyone else in the group cried, trembled, or looked as quietly resolved as I did. The counselor then responded, "Well, girls. I think we can all see that Shelley has had a difficult week, and I think it is best if we go ahead and end group today, so I can speak with her privately. See you next week." I sat motionless, staring at the ground. The counselor left the room for a moment then returned with an anti-suicide contract for me to sign. She read the document to me: "I, _____, promise not to harm myself in any way. If I feel the urge to commit suicide become overwhelming, I will go to the counseling office and seek assistance or dial 911..."

She explained that because I wasn't thinking clearly, I needed to make this commitment and sign my name on the sheet. I interpreted her remarks as patronizing due to my embittered state. As I grasped the bottom of the contract while she stood there holding the other end, I fired back at her: "If you want me to sign this form so that you can go home and eat dinner with your family without being legally liable for whatever I do, then fine. I will sign the sheet."

I signed the document and threw it at her with a string of profanities and stormed out of the counseling office. Arriving at my dorm room, I sat still for a few moments then flew into a rage. I pulled a metal rod out of the closet and began smashing every breakable object in the room whether it belonged to my roommate or me. I even took special care to crush several glass items against the wall with my bare hands.

When there was nothing left to break, I sat in a pile of shattered glass with a blank stare on my face and blood pouring down my hands. I then picked up two large pieces of glass and began grinding them into my hands. Only one thought was going through my mind: "How would I end this?"

Intervention

I had been planning to kill myself on my birthday. I was going to jump off my dormitory roof and fall into the stone courtyard, thus letting everyone know how unhappy I was to have ever been born, how angry I was, and how unwilling I was to accept the cards fate had dealt me. I would make the statement that unmistakably proved I had looked past life's façade and the sugarcoated words of a bumbling counselor with nothing to offer. I would refuse to play the game any further. As weary as I was, I was too alert to maintain any "light at the end of the tunnel" delusions. I would end it all with one self-determinant act of falling into a stone courtyard, where I would find bliss and relief from a sentence too long served.

The question now was, "Should I do it now or wait for my birthday?" That is what I was contemplating as I sat there in the pile of glass, grinding the shards into my hands and letting the blood drip onto the floor. I was measuring and meditating—measuring my misery and resigning myself to the fact that I may not make as bold a statement as I had hoped. I meditated on my plan one final time to make sure it was foolproof, then headed up the stairs to the top level of the dorm, hands still dripping with blood. One floor after another hailed me closer and closer to my final statement, my conclusion to the horror others had forced upon me.

I was quiet and resolute. There was no doubt in my mind, and I didn't feel any apprehension about what I was doing. The demonic stupor I was in made me think this was truly a wise choice. Like a robot, I followed what the evil one had been whispering to me for a long time, maybe even my whole life. How else could I rid myself of the shame of a little girl who had been viciously raped, sadistically tortured, and taught to believe she didn't deserve anything better? Each step took on a cadence—the sound of my breathing, the sound of each step echoing in the flights of stairs. Reaching the final floor I walked toward the small door I had climbed through during a previous rehearsal for my big day.

I was just eight or nine feet from the trap door that led to the roof, when seemingly out of nowhere a girl I had seen around campus was suddenly standing in front of me, stopping my progress. She caught me off guard with her simple greeting, "Hi, Shelley, how are you doing?" But it was as if I was in a trance. I stared over her head to the door handle that gave access to the roof and mumbled a weak "Hi."

Of course I must have been quite a sight, with blood dripping from my hands and broken glass still all over me. But either no one else had seen me or they had kept their distance. Now I was confronted with a living obstacle to the culmination of my plan. The girl's tone remained calm. "Shelley, it looks like there is blood on your hands. Let's go to the bathroom and wash your hands off." That's all she said. It wasn't profound, yet it was possibly the most life-altering statement ever made to me.

For some inexplicable reason, I looked down at my hands as if I was being awakened from a dream. I found myself turning around and walking toward the bathroom. I remember even looking over my shoulder up at the trap door and thinking,

"Why am I walking away from my goal?" And yet I couldn't get back on my course to the roof. Somehow I found myself in the bathroom as this acquaintance of mine washed the glass and blood off my hands. Then she said, "How about a walk outside? That would be good, wouldn't it?"

Again, inexplicably, I followed her until we were walking outside in the fresh fall weather. She began to ask me questions, and little by little I became more capable of talking again, as if I were waking from a stupor. My desire to kill myself was just as firm; my plan had just been derailed for the moment. She then asked me, "Shelley, is there anyone in the whole world whom you feel you could talk to right now?" I thought of a woman whom I had talked with in a very general way before I left for college and mentioned her name. My new friend packed an overnight bag and said, "OK, let's go."

To this day, I still can't understand how someone I didn't even know that well lured me from the roof when I was so determined to end my life. She canceled her classes and literally packed me into her car and drove me to see a counselor I had talked with when I was in high school. She was the only person I felt I could confide in. As soon as I got in the car with my friend, I wanted to rush back to my plan, back to the roof where I could finally find peace. I reached over to the door handle and tried to jump out of the car several times, but each time my friend prevented my escape.

Taking inventory of my new circumstances, I knew that accomplishing my goal might be in total jeopardy now that others were involved. My mind raced as I began to alter my plan to fit the new obstacles. I thought to myself, "I will act like I am not suicidal anymore. When we get to the counselor house, I will drum up an emotional confession, then say I am doing a lot better now and convince them I am fine so they will leave me alone. Then I can still achieve my plan."

By the time we arrived at the counselor's house, I was already beginning to play the part of a previously suicidal person who now realized she didn't want to make a decision like that. I was playing my part well, allowing my friend and the counselor to think they were gently persuading me to let go of my irrational thoughts of suicide. Yet while playing this role externally, I was consumed internally with only one thought. In every room I entered, I devised a way to kill myself with just about every object I laid eyes on. I only needed to be left alone for a moment. All of this was going on in my head while I let them think they were breaking through to me and that I was regaining rational thought—all so they would leave me alone.

After talking for a while in the living room, the counselor invited my friend and me into the kitchen to talk some more while she prepared dinner. As she cooked, she kept up a steady stream of conversation, and unbeknownst to me she was working a scheme of her own. Taking out a large butcher knife from the drawer, she began to chop up a salad in front of me. As she did so, she asked me, "So how are you feeling now in terms of those suicidal thoughts? Now that we have talked through some of what you are struggling with, do you feel less of an impulse to commit suicide? Do you think your desire to kill yourself has declined at this point?"

I answered with a phony sigh and the most remorseful

expression I could muster. "Yes, I don't know what I was thinking before. I guess I just got overwhelmed. Our conversation has really helped, and I am not in the same frame of mind anymore. I guess I just didn't feel like I had anyone to talk to or any way out. I didn't reach out for help or let people know how depressed I was really feeling. I know I have a long way to go in dealing with all of these emotions, but I do feel more able to cope now."

She continued cutting the vegetables and watched me out of the corner of her eye, careful not to demand my eyes to meet hers. Then she asked me again in a nonchalant tone, "So, you are not having suicidal thoughts?" I looked the part of a depressed-but-not-suicidal person. "No, I am not. I don't know what got into me before. In fact"—I turned to my friend—"I want to apologize for scaring everyone earlier at the college. I know that I don't want to give up and give in to those thoughts. I just felt so overwhelmed and forgot that I do have people I can reach out to. Honestly, I am not having the suicidal thoughts and urges I had before."

Right when I said that, the counselor chopped a few more slices of tomato then made an exaggerated gesture with the butcher knife, lifting it into the air from the cutting board, up past her face to the other side of her body, then back in front of her face, where her eyes met mine. I had been unintentionally following every movement of that knife since the moment she had taken it out of the drawer. Now, I was looking straight at her as she held the knife in front of her face.

Her eyes were intense and filled with awareness. She had me pinned. "Shelley! You have been lying to me since the moment you walked into my house. You are so obsessed with committing suicide you can't keep your eyes off of this knife or anything else you see in this house as a possible weapon. You are a danger to yourself, and I am giving you two options: one, you turn yourself in of your own volition to a psychiatric facility. Or two, I commit you to a psychiatric hospital involuntarily, which means you will be treated more strictly and will not have any input about when you will be released."

Caught, I felt there was only one thing I could do. I would say yes to the first option and hope to present myself to the hospital staff in a way that made them think the counselor had exaggerated my emotional state. I sat down in the living room while the only woman I thought I could confide in called the hospital in front of me. She told them some of my background and then calmly asked to speak with the counselor who would be evaluating me upon my arrival. I turned pale as I thought to myself, "No way! She is going to interfere with my plan again!"

Prayers in a Padded Room

Now speaking with the person in charge of evaluations and intake at the psychiatric facility, the counselor began to crush my hopes. "I want to let you know that the patient I am sending to you will present herself to be very calm and rational. She will probably even speak at length about how she was feeling suicidal but is better now and doesn't need to be admitted to the hospital but can simply follow up with counseling. She will look very cool, calm, and collected, but do not listen to a word she says. She will size up every room she enters for possible weapons to commit suicide. I have already caught her three times trying to kill herself in my house since she arrived."

I was enraged. I felt trapped with no options. I was escorted to the hospital under close watch, and my every attempt to harm myself was thwarted. Having already been briefed about me before I arrived, the counselors evaluated me and took every precaution when admitting me to the suicide ward of the hospital. This is when I first realized how bad things had gotten. The staff removed the drawstring from my sweatpants and took away my pens and shoelaces. Yet what was worse was the realization that, without a doubt, they needed to do this because I had already devised a plan to kill myself with my shoelaces. Arriving in my hospital room, I put my head in my hands and cried.

This was the lowest point of my life. After crying for a few moments, the anger that had been seeping out after a lifetime of suppressing my pain surged out in a wave. In an instant I was throwing chairs at the mirror and windows, which were, of course, shatterproof and impossible to break. The hidden surveillance camera picked up the whole scene, and within moments mental health workers were in my room, ushering me to the "quiet area."

The "QA" was a modern version of the padded room. The walls were padded, and there was a mattress on the floor, but there was absolutely nothing in the room I could use to harm myself. I remember sitting calmly for a moment and thinking to myself, "Well, if I was ever going to lose my mind it might as well be now. It's expected of me in this place anyway. I might as well go for it and give them a show."

Having located the small video cameras in the ceiling, I started running around the room in a circle, yelling at the top of my lungs, taking a few moments here and there to curse out the workers watching the whole charade through the hidden camera. I flipped them off with all kinds of gestures. Then I focused all my hatred and rage toward the minister and others who had abused and molested me as a child.

I let it all out. There was no pretense now. I don't know how long I continued in this manner; I just know that eventually I ran out of words, out of energy, out of profanity and vulgar gestures, out of new ways of cursing everyone who had wronged me. I had addressed each abuser by name, and in the most violent terms possible I had given voice to the seething rage that had been eating at me for so many years.

I collapsed onto the mattress, repulsed as much by my own anger as I had been by everyone who had hurt me so much. The exhausting exercise proved only one point: there was nothing left in me except rage, bitterness, and hatred. I knew once and for all, irrefutably, that there was nothing good in me—no light at the end of tunnel, no hope for Shelley Hundley.

No one could ask me to "dig deep" and "make it through somehow." I knew better. I could not be duped into thinking there was any amount of good in me, or that by any means I could rise up and conquer the evil that had defiled me to the core. No, there was nothing left. The abuse, the torture that only hell itself could give a name to, the memories that were just as lethal as the events themselves—they all had left me with a poison that ran so deep, everything in me had been tainted by it. No part of my being was shielded from its destruction.

As I lay there exhausted, a numbness seemed to fill me, and a vacant look came over my eyes. In that state, I lifted a clear and simple prayer. "If there is a God who can hear me," I whispered. "If there is a God who can hear me, if there is a God who can see me right now in the state I'm in, if You want me to live, You have to give me two things, or I cannot continue. I won't go on living this way.

"First, You have to prove to me beyond any doubt, just between You and me, that You are real. I can't take anyone else's word for it again. Second, if You prove Yourself to me, knowing that You exist is not enough. You have to show me that You can do something about this pain. Otherwise I vow right now that I will not live this way, and I will end my life the next chance I get."

The moment I uttered those "if there is a God" phrases, I didn't feel anything. I was so exhausted that I eventually fell asleep right there on the mattress. It would have seemed that my prayers were not answered, but God was setting some amazing things in motion that would ultimately save my life and bring me more joy than I could ever imagine.

Chapter Three

SEEING PAIN THROUGH
A NEW LENS

TODAY I OFTEN speak at the International House of Prayer in Kansas City, Missouri, and in churches across the nations. After hearing my testimony, sometimes people approach me and say, "Well, my suffering is not as great as yours, but..." I always stop them there. God does not rate suffering on different scales and compare the feelings of one with those of another. The Bible shows us a vast array of suffering that came in all sorts of packages. Every human being has experienced pain. It is one currency we all share. My journey certainly has been filled with pain, but by God's grace I have come to see suffering in a new light. Whether it is the wound of abuse or the disappointment of believing for but not yet receiving a physical healing, suffering puts humanity on a level playing field and points us to the one pain that is common to us all—our need for God to break into our lives and make the wrong things right. At its most basic level, every pain we experience reveals a longing within us to encounter God's beauty, or the essence of who He is. For some, that beauty is found in knowing the depth of the Father's love for us. For others, it is recognizing the great delight He takes in us. Because of the ravaging effects of sin, we are often unable to rightly discern beauty. We try to fill those longings for love and meaning with so many other things—careers, relationships, material possessions.

As we chase after these lesser "beauties," we neglect the One who is ultimate beauty, the One who truly can meet our deepest need. As 2 Corinthians 4:4 says, "The god of this age has blinded the minds of unbelievers, so that they cannot see the light of the gospel of the glory of Christ, who is the image of God" (NIV). (See also Isaiah 53:2; Romans 1:21; and Ephesians 1:18; 4:17–18.) If left to simply chase after beauty according to our own attraction, we will inevitably worship everything around us, even ourselves, and never realize the superior beauty that only God possesses. This is where pain becomes our invitation into the heart of God. Without pain, we would remain fascinated by one vanity after another. Pain reveals to us the inadequacy of what we are beholding and unlocks our ache for a greater beauty to fulfill our need. Pain and suffering, therefore, are useful not because they have redemptive or transforming power, but because of what they tear down in our lives and the One to whom they can lead us. Pain directs us to the place where God is waiting, ready to change us.

It is for this reason that God's plan laid out in the Book of Revelation involves pain on a devastatingly wide scale. He knows pain to be the best tutor to lead a spiritually blind and deaf world to the saving knowledge of Jesus Christ. Somehow the places of our hearts that are blind to beauty are within the reach of pain. When pain hits us, we reach beyond our surroundings, beyond ourselves, and become vulnerable enough to be changed by the true beauty of Christ. Pain speaks loudly, even to the deaf, and draws us into intimacy with the Father. As C. S. Lewis wrote in *The Problem of Pain*, "God whispers to us in our pleasures, speaks in our conscience, but shouts in our pains: it is his megaphone to rouse a deaf world."[1]

These are just some of the ways pain works to lead us to the place where the beauty of Jesus can transform us:

- Pain causes us to realize that our hearts are alive.

- Pain gives us an indication of how much beauty we have seen.

- Pain reveals the depth of our emotional capacity.

- Pain shatters our phony attachments and faulty dependencies.

- Pain has the ability to change our priorities in a moment.

- Pain is persistent and will not be deceived.

- Rather than disqualifying us from intimacy with God, pain escorts us into it.

- Instead of keeping us from the knowledge of God, pain is the place where we encounter it most deeply.

God can use pain to accomplish His work, but that does not mean that pain and suffering are inherently good, as some throughout history have suggested. I wholeheartedly reject this notion. Pain will be an economy only on this side of the human experience; God does not use pain as an escort in the age to come. God hates pain and suffering (Deut. 26:5-8; Isa. 63:9). He even promises in Revelation 21:4 that there will be no more tears or pain in heaven.

Pain and suffering are inherently destructive and cannot change us by themselves. We see widespread suffering in many nations of the world, yet we do not necessarily see those countries shining with redemptive glory. Many of us have seen disease or intense suffering devour individuals, robbing them of their dignity and strength as human beings. Much of the earth is burdened with afflictions that have led them only to hate and accuse God. Experiencing pain and suffering does *not* guarantee spiritual maturity. The poor, broken, and suffering are not more like Jesus due to their experiences; rather, they have great potential if they turn to Jesus in the midst of their pain.

God's exchange rate in the midst of suffering is great. One moment of pain that is turned into a loving exchange with Jesus through prayer and meditation upon His Word has the potential to transform us more than a thousand moments of blessing and privilege. The last thing God wants is for us to feel capable of managing our lives on our own and fail to cleave to Him through our pain.

The nation of Israel certainly saw this to be true. Ancient Israel struggled the most spiritually in times of blessing, then often turned back to God when trials came. We are called to draw near to God in the midst of adversity as well as in times of blessing. Please know that while we need to be equipped to deal with pain when it comes knocking, there is no need for us to search for more suffering as some mistakenly did throughout church history. The mature bride of Christ knows that both the north winds of adversity and the south winds of blessing (Song of Sol. 4:16) are necessary in order for God to release the fragrance that is most pleasing to Him, the fragrance of Christ (2 Cor. 2:15).

Pictures of Suffering

In the Bible, we see God dignifying those who suffer and sharing in their pain. He points us all to the great joy that is to come as well as giving us supernatural grace to triumph over our suffering. I believe that one of the most helpful skills we can develop as believers is the ability to meet Jesus in our own pain, therefore being able to lead others to Him in theirs. In Scripture, there is much diversity in the ways people suffer and in God's purpose for the affliction.

Examining five pictures of suffering in the Bible may give you some insight into God's purpose for allowing your pain. It also will reveal some keys to help you endure pain without losing faith that God is at work in the midst of it. When we meet the Lord through our heartache and the blindfold of our own fallen understanding is removed, we will experience what we can now only hope for in faith.

1. God uses pain to bring us back to our first love.

In Hosea 2:1-20, we see God dealing with the nation of Israel and answering their prayer to know Him not only as their master but also as their husband. In jealous love, He strips away every prop and leaves Israel slain with thirst and unable to find her other lovers (Hosea 2:3–5), which causes her to return to her first love. As believers, God shakes our lives at times to answer the very prayers we have prayed. He always uses the least severe means to remove what is hindering our intimacy with Him. I liken this to a loving father whose child has cancer. Although the child may not understand why he is experiencing the pain of needles, chemotherapy, or surgery, his loving father allows the doctor to do his work. Jesus sometimes permits suffering and shaking in our lives because there is a more dangerous cancer lurking deep within that He needs to bring to the surface and remove.

2. God uses suffering to prepare His deliverers for His work.

Suffering took an interesting twist in the life of Joseph. As we read in Genesis 37-45, Joseph had great favor before the Lord, but his life took a dark turn when his own family betrayed him. Having been sold into slavery by his brothers, Joseph was left to wonder whether the dreams God gave him about the calling on his life would ever come to pass. Yet as Joseph's journey continued, the very thing his brothers meant for his harm became the tool God used to position

Joseph to save thousands of lives, including his own family. (See Genesis 45:5-8.)

When I read accounts like Joseph's, I am reminded of a statement Teresa of Avila made in fifteenth-century Spain. She said, "Lord, if this is the way You treat Your friends, it's no wonder You have so few!"[2] God certainly does use suffering to train His friends and prepare those He has called to bring deliverance to the captives. This is a truth I discovered several years ago when I was diagnosed with a chronic and debilitating sickness.

In 1999 I served with a handful of people who, under the leadership of Mike Bickle, began the International House of Prayer in Kansas City, Missouri. A short time after we started this ministry, I was diagnosed with Crohn's disease and went through almost four years of major sickness. During that time, I was hospitalized at least one week every month before I received a miraculous healing and a complete reversal of the diagnosis.

When I first realized that I was entering into a battle regarding my health, I had a conversation with Mike, and I still remember his words so vividly. He said, "Shelley, there is no question that this sickness comes from the evil one as he is raging against the calling God has placed on your life. Yet God will use the very limitations and suffering that this sickness imposes on you to be the setting in which you receive the greatest preparation and breakthrough into your calling. This will be God's seminary for you, and I have no doubt you will come out of this with a breakthrough of healing, yet also prepared and released into your calling."

Those words proved to be so true! Much of what I am sharing in this book and what I tell my classes at the International House of Prayer University comes from the season of study, meditation, and suffering I endured during those years on my sickbed.

3. God uses suffering to reveal His glory.

The Bible's best-known example of suffering is Job. Much like he did with Peter in Luke 22:31–32, Satan asked God for permission to sift Job. God allowed Satan access to His friend, putting Job on display and ultimately revealing His great glory.

> Now there was a day when the sons of God came to present themselves before the LORD, and Satan also came among them. And the LORD said to Satan, "From where do you come?" So Satan answered the LORD and said, "From going to and fro on the earth, and from walking back and forth on it." Then the LORD said to Satan, "Have you considered My servant Job, that there is none like him on the earth, a blameless and upright man, one who fears God and shuns evil?" So Satan answered the LORD and said, "Does Job fear God for nothing? Have You not made a hedge around him, around his household, and around all that he has on every side? You have blessed the work of his hands, and his possessions have increased in the land. But now, stretch out Your hand and touch all that he has, and he will surely curse You to Your face!" And the LORD said to Satan, "Behold, all that he has is in your power;

only do not lay a hand on his person." So Satan went
out from the presence of the LORD.

—JOB 1:6–12

We will never understand the inner workings of this
conversation between God and Satan on this side of eternity,
but we can learn much from the story of Job. It has become
the inspiration for every believer who knows how to thank
God in times of blessing but is challenged to praise Him just
as much when everything seems to go wrong. We also get a
glimpse into the mysterious fact that no matter what we are
going through, we are truly on display. Heaven is watching
to see how we respond, and so are many people here on the
earth. Our impact is much greater than we perceive.

This really means something in the moment of suffering,
especially for those dealing with physical sickness and
awaiting God's healing. Perhaps the biggest discouragement
is the feeling of being inhibited from having real impact for
Jesus during our time of illness and pain. Suffering for a cause
has some level of glory in it, but suffering that seems mean-
ingless can be the greatest torment of all. While sick with
Crohn's disease for those years, I was challenged by some
phenomenal friends to see the impact my weak "yes" to God
was having on His heart and those around me. Unbeknownst
to me, people were watching me, and they received strength
and encouragement by seeing me reach out to God and continue to trust and believe Him in the midst of such difficulty.

4. God uses pain to prepare God's people to reign.

In Daniel 7:9-14, the prophet has a powerful vision of "the Ancient of Days," our heavenly Father, seated on His throne. He has all power and all authority, and there is fire around His throne and ten thousand times ten thousand angels standing before Him. God is totally in charge, and He has a mysterious plan in His heart—He wants to give His kingdom to His beloved Son. Ezekiel 1:26 also reveals this glorious plan, as it shows Jesus seated in the center of the throne. Psalm 2 tells the same story from the perspective of the nations of the earth, who receive their rightful ruler, King Jesus. In Daniel 7:27, we learn that the kingdom will ultimately be given to the saints of the Most High God. The bride of Christ—those who accept Jesus as Savior—will rule and reign with Him.

Yet in light of all this triumph, there is suffering. Daniel sees God on His throne with all power. He sees the Father giving all authority to His Son and His Son giving the kingdom and the right to rule and reign with Him to His people. But the big surprise comes in the method God uses to bring this plan into fruition. He raises up an adversary (called the Antichrist in the Book of Revelation) and allows His people to endure unprecedented persecution as a means of preparing His bride to rule and reign with Him. God's plan regarding suffering in the Book of Revelation is quite a paradigm shift in our understanding. It reveals again that God knows something about pain and suffering and how it can be used in a limited way to shake His people, bring forth His love in us, and prepare us to walk in the authority He longs to share with us. He wants us to be equally yoked with Christ in love so much that He raises up an adversary to train us in voluntary love. As Christ's bride, the church overcomes only by being victorious in love (Rev. 12:11). The adversary will overcome her physically, resulting in martyrdom, but she will triumph spiritually, receiving the right to rule with Jesus forever. (To further study the martyrdom and suffering described in Daniel and Revelation, see Daniel 7:21, 25; 8:24; 11:33–25; 12:7, 10; Revelation 6:9–11; 13:7; 17:6; 18:24; 19.)

5. Suffering gives God access to the deepest places of our hearts.

God's presence is always with us, but we can't always feel it. It is in the moment of greatest darkness, when we are barraged with every reason not to believe and trust, that Jesus gives a simple command that is the most difficult thing for a suffering heart to do. He simply says, "Open for me" (Song of Sol. 5:2). Throughout her journey described in the Song of Solomon, the bride of Christ is given many commands—to arise, run over mountains, go out to the vineyard and labor, and so on. But when His bride is suffering, Christ has only one request—that she respond to His knocking and open the deepest places of her heart to Him.

In Song of Solomon 5:2, we see a picture of Jesus coming to His bride with His hair wet from the night dew. This speaks of Jesus's own suffering in the Garden of Gethsemane and His invitation for us to meet Him in the place of suffering. When the bride responds to His knock, she cannot find Him. During this time when she could not feel His presence, the bride is given an opportunity to tell less mature believers (referred to figuratively in Song of Solomon 5:16 as "daughters of Jerusalem") how beautiful Jesus is to her and why she is so lovesick for Him.

Reading Song of Solomon, it is easy to pick up on the bride's passion for the Bridegroom as she recalls attributes of Jesus she can no longer see. After the bride's declaration of His beauty, Jesus proclaims in poetic language how touched and impacted God is when He is loved and adored in those times of darkness and suffering when we cannot see Him or feel His presence.

> O my love, you are as beautiful as Tirzah, lovely as Jerusalem, awesome as an army with banners! Turn your eyes away from me, for they have overcome me.
> —SONG OF SOLOMON 6:4–5

In this verse, we see a picture of just how deeply it moves Jesus to see someone who, in her moment of suffering, is able to remember the beauty of who He is and declare it to others. Armies cannot conquer Jesus, hell's demons cannot defeat Him, the wealth and might of all of the nations of the earth cannot overwhelm Him, but one reality can captivate Him— love from a suffering heart.

This passage took on special meaning for me when I battled through my years of sickness. When I went to bed each night, I would imagine Jesus leaning over the balcony of heaven in anticipation of how Shelley Hundley would respond to Him in her hour of intense suffering. I would lie there on my bed and whisper: "Jesus, I know that You didn't heal me again today, but I also know what You are longing for as You look at my heart. I know what I can give You now in this darkness that won't be the same after You have healed me and I can see You clearly for who You are. I can love you! Jesus, in the midst of all that I am going through, the pain and my inability to sense Your presence, I love You!"

I then would imagine my heavenly Bridegroom speaking the same words to me: "Shelley, you are so beautiful to Me right now. You are awesome! You are overcoming the accusations and fears like an army triumphing in battle. Turn your eyes away from Me. It's too much for Me! I am overcome."

With a playful smile on my face and tears in my eyes, I often ended those days saying, "Jesus, it's hard for You, isn't it? Yes, I know it must be difficult for You to go even one more day without healing me when You see how much I love You right now." During my time of sickness, I went through that whole conversation almost every night before I went to sleep, and I gained so much strength as I saw Jesus do a deep work in my heart. Those truly were my seminary years. In the dark night of suffering, when we feel nothing, He feels every little movement of our hearts and is able to do so much in us and even through us.

My Response to Suffering is a Gift

Sometimes in the midst of sickness or suffering, we need to feel the impact of what we are doing in our hearts before Jesus and how the internal choices we make are influencing others. Realizing that my suffering could become a gift helped me steady my own heart in the midst of my time of sickness. This is what the Holy Spirit taught me:

My response to suffering is a gift to Jesus.

For all of eternity we will be face-to-face with the beauty and splendor of our God, but only during my lifetime on the earth do I have the opportunity to impact the heart of God in the midst of darkness, accusation, and blindness. I have a chance only today to love Him in the midst of my current hardships, for this is when my heart feels nothing and sees nothing, but still I move in love toward the One I cannot see. And His heart is most undone. I feel nothing, but He feels everything!

My response to suffering is a gift to a hurting generation.

I long not only to see people delivered but also to offer them the gold I have mined in the secret place of suffering where I have discovered how to receive God's beauty for my ashes (Isa. 61:3). This generation is longing for a gospel that frees them from their chains. They are seeking a God who sees their tears and vindicates their pain. I want to stand before this generation and release the anointing to turn pain into intimacy with the Father.

My response to suffering is a gift to the body of Christ.

When I consider the crisis of future suffering that awaits the earth before the Lord's return, God's ways with me seem extremely appropriate. My trials seem like mild tremors of a future upheaval sent by a wise God. He is raising up voices to prepare the body of Christ for the coming time of suffering before the Lord returns. Anything that prepares me to not be offended on that painful day and to teach others to do the same seems wise! Oh, that we would have hearts that are easily escorted into love in the midst of pain. Could there be any gift more appropriate for the body of Christ in this generation? By turning to Him in and through our trials, we are buying a gold more precious than anything we could imagine. When we understand that the greatest invitation of pain and suffering is able to lead us back to our loving, beautiful Bridegroom, our hearts will move toward Him in the midst of our pain, and we will lead others to do the same.

A Witness to a Lost and Dying World

Some years ago, I was at a café-bookstore and struck up a conversation with a worker I met there. I began to share my testimony with her and made every effort to win her to Christ. For the next several months we stayed in contact by phone, and I visited her at the café and at an art museum where she also worked. In our conversations, she shared her own horrendous experience growing up in a religious sect that encouraged all manner of sexual abuse and exploration. Her background left her in a pursuit of true spirituality as she had dabbled in everything from New Age to Buddhism to the occult.

Before meeting me she had been most impressed with Buddhism, which seemed to help her make sense of her suffering. As I told her about my relationship with Jesus, the Holy Spirit began to soften her heart toward the gospel. I felt prompted by the Lord to allow this young woman to ask me any questions she wanted about my past and what Jesus has done in the deepest places of my pain.

Talking with her on the phone one night, I told her about

forgiveness and how we can give Jesus our ashes and receive from Him peace and deep joy in exchange. I have lived this reality and was confident she could experience it too, but still I didn't realize how my testimony was affecting her. She told me, "It's like you are a professor of pain. I have never met anyone more comfortable with what they have been through, sensitive to theirs and others' pains, and more authentic in their spirituality. It's like you know more about pain than anyone I have met, yet you seem happier than anyone I have talked with. You have been through more pain and suffering, but there is this happy glow about you." Her observations helped me realize the profound impact of God's redemptive work in my life.

This generation is filled with people who are broken, and they need hope and healing. They have suffered so much and have been ravaged by perversion and exploitation on so many levels. Humanity seems to have lost all restraint. Rape and abuse have become common. Human beings behave as though there are no boundaries on how they can fulfill their desires. They violently exploit others in the pursuit of their own pleasure.

The young woman I met was a victim of this very perversion, but she didn't even seem to recognize it as such. Influenced by our relativistic culture, she categorized her abuse as an "exploratory experience" that was neither wrong nor right. She did not connect any of it to her dysfunctional pattern of sexual immorality. When I asked about her experience and offered some thoughts about how the pain and trauma had affected her, she was stunned by my perspective and surprised by the way I dealt with similar pain in my own life.

Encountering Jesus through our pain equips us to help a lost and hurting generation looking to make sense of their suffering. Praise God, we know the One who can give them beauty for ashes. If I had taken shortcuts or refused to confront my pain, I wouldn't have been comfortable addressing someone else's suffering. My witness would have seemed shallow to this young woman, and she would have tuned me out as she had done so many others who had witnessed to her previously.

I am convinced that how we approach pain as believers will directly affect our witness to the lost. They are weighed down with so much sorrow that they turn to drugs, immorality, and false religions to cope. As followers of Jesus, we have the capacity to offer hope to a world in pain all around us—if we would only allow ourselves to meet God in our own private place of pain.

Chapter Four

PIERCING THE HARDEST HEART

W HEN I WAS sitting in the padded room of the psychiatric hospital, I prayed for the first time in months,
asking God to reveal Himself to me. I wanted Him to prove
His existence beyond the shadow of a doubt, and I wanted
Him to show me that He could do something about the deep
pain I was enduring. In the moment of that prayer, it seemed
like nothing happened, but later I found out God had been
up to something after all.

During those very days, a small group of students who
had been filled with the Holy Spirit and were fasting and
praying for revival on my college campus began to target me
at a whole new level. While reading through several journals
of revivalists, the students had come upon William Booth's
advice for bringing about revival. Booth advocated the tactic
of finding the "hardest heart" and focusing prayers and out-
reach on the person whom no one expected to accept Christ.

These students caught a vision to reach the hardest heart
and watch that one soul bring many others in its wake,
leading to full-scale revival. I am sure that there were several
people identified, but because of my foul language and antag-
onism toward Christians who tried to witness to me, it's not

hard to imagine how my name might have ended up at the top of their list of hard hearts.

After ten days in the hospital and some serious doses of antidepressants, I was released from the psychiatric facility. The campus mental health center assigned me a new counselor named Lesley Westberry. She not only was more experienced in dealing with the combination of sexual and sadistic abuse I had experienced, but I would later find out that she also was an on-fire, Spirit-filled believer. At this same time, the little group of radical followers of Jesus began to rally together in prayer for me.

These students attempted to share the love of Christ with me again and again. In return I cursed at them, vomiting descriptions of what I had endured that were so vulgar, most of them were left backing away from me in tears. Still, they kept coming back, showing up in my classes and in the hallways to tell me about Jesus. I had no idea that my weak prayers in a padded hospital room had put a heavenly bull's-eye on me and that these young intercessors would not take no for an answer.

During this time, I went through another stint of depression as some new horrific memories surfaced. One day while I was in the school cafeteria, a smell or sound, I'm still not sure which, sent me into post-traumatic shock as horrible memories flooded my mind. I made it back to my dorm room, where I began to sob uncontrollably. Before long, I was curled up in a fetal position hyperventilating. As my mind filled with images of the abuse, I began to feel the excruciating pain in my body. As the memory continued, the emotional and physical pain became too much.

My body, which had been shaking and wracked with pain as I relived the worst scene of my past abuse, suddenly became motionless and numb. Every muscle in my body relaxed, my whimpering and sobbing came to an immediate and eerie halt, and my eyes became vacant. I sat there on the bed staring blankly at the nearest wall, barely breathing. My mouth hung open with saliva dripping down. I was no longer swallowing, and my eyes were hardly even blinking. My shallow breaths seemed to be the only signs of life.

The Brink of Death

I don't remember much, but I was told that friends came into the room, saw me in this state, and tried to rouse me to no avail. Eventually the resident director of the dorm was called in, but still there was no response or movement from me. About an hour into my total breakdown, my counselor was paged from her family vacation. Gathering information from those who had been with me before I entered this coma-like state, Lesley hypothesized that the memories had been so traumatic they had induced a catatonic state. This could lead to a permanent emotional coma from which I might never recover.

With the paramedics on standby to take me to the hospital, Lesley began trying to bring me back to reality. She gave specific instructions to friends and school counselors who were nearby. They described to her every detail of my surroundings—which way I was facing, what was in front of me, what ambient sounds were present in the room—and

Lesley asked them to put the phone by my ear for five-minute periods then give me a break and tell her if I made movements of any kind.

Lesley began with soothing and very slow speech. I remember beginning to hear her voice as if it were far away but still being unable to pull myself out of this catatonic state. "Shelley, this is Lesley. You are sitting on a bed right now. Can you feel the mattress that you are sitting on?" Then there was a break before she spoke again. "Shelley, this is Lesley. You are looking at a blue-colored wall right now. I want you to focus on that wall that's in front of you. Can you see it?"

Lesley continued to tug on me slowly. She followed her professional training, though she had no assurance it would work. She patiently kept tugging on me phrase by phrase, trying to pull me back to a reality that to me seemed too deadly to risk existing in. "Shelley, this is Lesley. I want you to listen now for your own breathing. Can you hear it? Shelley, can you feel and hear your breathing? I know you have experienced a lot of pain, but you are still breathing. Shelley, if you can hear and feel your breathing, I want you to blink your eyes for me. Shelley, can you do that? Can you blink your eyes? No one is going to force you to do anything. We are going to make sure you are safe. Can you blink your eyes for me?"

There was no movement from me, then suddenly a faint blinking of the eye, then one more a little stronger. "Yes! She's coming back. Oh, thank God," stammered the dormitory resident director to Lesley on the phone. After thirty to forty minutes on the phone with me, somehow Lesley had succeeded in reengaging me with the world. The resident director pressed the phone against my ear a final time. Lesley said to me, "Shelley, good job. You are doing so well. You don't need to explain anything to anyone. I know you feel very tired right now. It's fine for you to just lie down now, OK?" I seemed to come back to myself. I looked around the room at the concerned little crowd that had gathered around me. I laid down on the bed as some friends stretched a blanket over me. I was exhausted. Lesley explained to the others, "Just let her sleep now. Let's pray hard that she wakes up fully conscious and able to speak and communicate. She is not out of the woods yet, but there is a good chance that we did get her back since she was able to respond to me and blink. All we can do is pray and let her get some rest."

I did wake up the next day, and though I was not ready to describe all the memories that had flooded back the previous day, I was able to talk. I was also filled with another fierce desire to kill myself and was found slicing my hands with razors. The urge to commit suicide was very strong, but this time some part of me still wanted to live. I turned myself in to the nearby state psychiatric hospital. This was one of the oldest psychiatric hospitals in the country, and its conditions at that time left a lot to be desired. In fact, the very next year it was completely overhauled and placed under new management. I was admitted into a general ward of men and women, some of whom were beginning life sentences in the hospital due to murder, sexual assault, or decades of untreated mental illness. The hospital was more like a very dangerous jail with hardly any supervision and no real treatment.

Due to my previous suicide attempts, I was not allowed to be in a room for fear that I might find a way to harm myself. Without any monitoring technology, the hospital staff had no recourse but to have me sleep in a hospital bed in the hallway. All night long I lay there terrified of being sexually assaulted by the many violent men who constantly attacked people in plain view, with little interference from the staff. For the most part, the hospital workers stayed in an office enclosure made of shatterproof glass, leaving their office only to administer drugs, put someone in a straitjacket, or strap a violent patient to his bed when his behavior became too dangerous. Otherwise, the patients had to protect themselves.

I made it through this hospital stay without incurring any physical harm, but I was terrified my entire time there. However, the whole experience had one interesting effect on me. After seeing society's most vulnerable psychological cases, I began to think, "Wow, I don't feel as crazy as the people around me. I may make it after all." I didn't understand it at the time, but I felt as though someone somehow had preserved me. I remember my one and only visit with a psychologist at the facility. As she sat across the table from me, she closed my very thick file, leaned forward looking straight at me, and said in long, drawn-out tones, "*Helloooo, Shelley. Howwww are yooou?*" It was easy to see that she didn't expect me to be able to speak at all and was quite surprised by my cheeky, profanity-laden response.

After asking me some questions about the severity of my depression and suicidal thoughts (which at this point I was more honest about), she said, "Can I ask you one more question? You see, your abuse coupled with the violence in your surroundings as a child puts you in the company of only two other people we have ever seen hospitalized here. One just couldn't cope anymore and is in a complete emotional coma. She can't speak and never will. You may have seen her in the back room. The other is a man who is irrecoverably violent with no sense of humanity in him at all.

"When I see and interact with you, I can see the effects of the abuse you have undergone. But somehow it seems like the center of who you are has not been completely obliterated as one would expect. It seems you have survived the worst and that somehow you will make it. Can you explain why you are affected but not totally obliterated by the traumas you have experienced?"

At this point, I was still an avowed atheist. Yet I sighed and said, "Look, I don't believe any of it right now, but I am sure I will at some point admit that it is because of Jesus Christ." The woman's eyes filled with tears, and our appointment was over. All I could think was, "Why on earth did I say that?"

A Holy Spirit Target

Meanwhile, the small group of college students continued to barrage heaven with their prayers on my behalf. Their faculty adviser taught my Western Civilizations history class, and there was something about him that intrigued me. I couldn't put my finger on it, but he seemed genuine, and for whatever reason I just couldn't dismiss this teacher.

I had missed a lot of classes and was in quite a bit of

trouble in school. Severe depression and hospitalizations had taken their toll, and the majority of my teachers seemed to have already given up on me, but this professor was different. He badgered me for prayer requests and seemed to have a personal interest in how I was doing.

We'd never had any personal conversations, and I kept him in the dark on what was really going on. I blamed all of my absences on medical issues, which wasn't completely untrue. I was having major problems with hyperthyroidism and a heart condition that was becoming even worse due to all of the emotional stress I was under. But I had made a habit of lying to my professors about late papers, missed classes, and my notorious absences at the college's required chapel services.

One Saturday halfway through the second semester of my sophomore year, the phone in my dorm room rang. To my surprise, my history professor was calling. My mind went immediately to the paper I had lied to him about and the phony excuse I had given for missing class. I couldn't help but think that if I fell out of favor with this professor, I might get kicked out of college, and that was a bad prospect even in my state of mind. If I weren't in college, I didn't know where I would go. I knew from experience how horrible psychiatric hospitals could be, and home was only slightly more appealing as the first round of conversations with my family about my abuse did not go well at all.

The professor didn't waste any time letting me know why he called. "Shelley, I was praying this morning and preparing for the Saturday night Bible study I lead at my house each week, and God spoke to me." I had already heard enough. *God* spoke to him? I had grown up around ministers, but no one I knew used that kind of religious language. In fact, my first thought was, "Wait a minute. Can't you go to hell for saying that?" Then, of course, I had to remind myself that I didn't believe in hell. Undaunted by my awkward silence, he continued to speak. "Shelley, I was praying, and God told me that you are to come tonight. God is going to heal your body and touch your heart."

He was speaking of the hyperthyroidism, which had become so bad the doctors were planning to radiate my entire thyroid gland and put me on iodine pills for the rest of my life. Although I didn't like the prospects I was facing, my professor's words left me flabbergasted. I didn't think people talked this way. What was he thinking, and why on earth would he ever think I would attend his Bible study? Here I was, a student who couldn't stand sitting through chapel services, who cursed out everyone who even dared to bring up the name of Jesus, and who vowed to never again hear any teaching from the Bible if I could help it.

Yet he was inviting me not only to a Bible study but also to a group that all the students and faculty knew to be the most off-balanced, fanatical, "Spirit-filled" Christians on campus. Was he kidding me? Of course I wouldn't go! I don't have a theological explanation for what happened next; I am simply going to tell it as it occurred. I opened my mouth to say no and give an excuse that would sound legitimate enough not to make any waves. Instead I heard myself say, "Yes. Thank you. I will come. Can you give me directions?"

Standing next to me was a friend who at the time was as far away from God as I was. She was waving frantically at me, mouthing, "What are you doing?" I had no explanation. I seemed to be in some kind of mental fog. The next thing I knew, I was writing down directions to his Bible study. Hanging up the phone, I came back to myself in an instant and couldn't believe what I had done. Now I felt trapped. I was in too much trouble to renege on my promise at this point. I was stuck!

Seeing that I had to go, I came up with a foolproof plan. I would arrive at the very end of the meeting. Expecting the format to be like what I was accustomed to growing up, I thought the meeting would have a few opening hymns, a sermon of some kind, then a closing hymn. Not caring to ever hear the Bible taught again as long as I lived, I was aiming for the closing hymn, not realizing that charismatic Bible studies were quite different from the church services I attended as a child. Unbeknownst to me, my plan meant that I would actually be arriving when the meeting was at its hottest—after the teaching, when the Holy Spirit was ministering to people.

The moment I walked in the room I knew this was unlike any church I had ever visited. I had planned to make my entrance, nod to my professor, then head out of there as quickly as possible. I literally had a friend waiting in the car to help me make a speedy getaway. But upon walking in the door, I was completely surprised by what I saw. There were people with their hands raised and their eyes closed, completely immersed in what they were doing. I noticed some others kneeling and crying with a look of love and devotion on their faces, as if they were singing and praying to a real person. Still others were jumping, dancing, or laughing with joy.

The scene caught me completely off guard. I remember thinking, "Wow! If everything people claimed to believe about Jesus was really true, it would make more sense for Christians to act like this instead of the lifeless way I have seen people behave in the church." Then I quickly discarded the thought, reminding myself that I didn't believe any of this religious mumbo jumbo. As I continued to look around the room, I realized something else. All of the students who had been pestering me the most about Jesus, who wouldn't let up in their evangelism, seemed to be in this one room. It was then that I actually got scared. It felt like a conspiracy. In truth, I had just uncovered the headquarters of our campus's most fiery believers, and they had been targeting me for quite some time in prayer.

I looked for my professor to give him a quick nod of acknowledgment, hoping I could then leave as quickly as I came in. However, as soon as I saw him, he quieted the worship leader and said, "Shelley Hundley is here tonight!" The room erupted with a chorus of "Hallelujah!" and "Praise the Lord." I will never forget one guy yelling out, "God told me He would give me her soul tonight!" I was terrified by this statement and wasn't sure if I wanted to know how he would go about getting my soul.

Scared and thrown off of my foolproof plan, I soon realized that the people gathering around me were preventing my quick exit. My professor smiled at me and said, "Shelley, can we pray for you?" Growing up in a conservative denomination, I always thought the statement "we will be praying for you" was simply something people said at the close of a church service, whether they planned to do so or not. I smiled thinking somehow I had to get myself out of this mess. I replied, "Yes. Sure, pray for me." Then came the surprises.

Jesus Answers

The professor pulled a chair into the center of the room and asked me to sit in it. What was this "sit in the chair" stunt? I thought I was merely telling everyone good-bye. I felt that I had no choice at this point, so I walked to the center of the room and sat down in the chair. The students gathered around, laid hands on me, and began to pray. I cringed through the whole experience. At this stage of my life, I did not like people touching me at all, let alone "laying on hands," which I had never experienced before.

One girl I had often seen on campus and to whom I had been nothing but rude, knelt on the floor with her hand on my shoe. I thought to myself, "OK, one thing is certain. My shoe does not need prayer!" The whole experience was thrusting me so far out of my comfort zone I can't overstate how awkward I felt. In that basement room, I was surrounded by the very students who had been badgering me about Jesus since I arrived at college. I kept thinking, "I will never humiliate myself like this again. I can't even tolerate the mildly religious students on my campus, much less subject myself to the fanatics in their very headquarters."

I closed my eyes and threatened heaven with one statement:

"God, if You exist at all, You better reveal Yourself now because I will never humiliate myself like this again." I have thought often about this statement over the years, and I am so ashamed of the arrogant tone I lobbed toward heaven in what I imagine to be the worst salvation prayer ever prayed. In fact, I'm not even sure it could be called a salvation prayer. Yet Jesus perceived the tiny cracking open of the door of my heart and put His foot right in there, saying, "I'll take it. Father, can I go? May I reveal Myself to her?"

To my utter shock, Jesus responded to me that night. As soon as I thrust this prideful thought up toward heaven, I felt a weighty presence descend and rest on me. I can only describe it as the glory of God. I couldn't move or speak. I became totally unaware of anyone around me or anything going on in the room. I didn't see a vision of any kind, but I felt that I was alone in a room with God Himself. Every fiber of my being knew that He was real, that He was present, and that He could do whatever He wanted to do with me. I also knew He would be justified in anything He did. It was terrifying and enthralling all at once. I felt remorse and regret at the very deepest level imaginable. In that moment, I knew without a doubt that God was real and that I was in His presence. I realized how wrong I had been to judge the living God by the human beings who had hurt me or by the bitterness I had allowed to build up in my heart. I didn't just feel sorry for the wrong things I had done or thought about God. It was so much more than that. I knew at the core of my being that I was completely, profoundly, and irreparably wrong. Unable to move under the weight of His presence, I experienced what I now know to be the fear of the Lord.

Clarity seemed to come to me for the first time in my life. I knew God could do whatever He wanted with me and He would be right in all of His actions. If He decided to take the breath right out of me, He would be justified. This was either the best news I had ever heard or the worst; I wasn't sure which. But my first question from the padded room in the psychiatric hospital asking God to prove His existence to me had been answered. I could never deny the reality of God again. However, my second question still remained. I knew God was real, but could He do something about my pain? I was not so naïve to think I could survive the devastation that ran so much deeper than I could articulate. If nothing could be done about the pain, I simply would not make it.

It seemed as if I was sitting in that chair motionless under the weight and reality of God's presence for a really long time, but it couldn't have been more than several minutes. I felt like I was dangling off a cliff, waiting to see what God would do and whether His existence was good or bad news to me. Soon, I felt the weight of God's glory slowly begin to lift as I became aware of the people around me praying. They began to tell me things about my childhood and to describe pictures they were seeing that pierced my heart with their poignancy. These college students whom I had mistreated so many times were giving details about my past that I had never told anyone.

As one by one they shared the things they felt Jesus was telling them, I became completely undone. Tears began to stream down my face, not just because of their words, but because of the love I felt from them. God was screaming to me through them, "Shelley, I know you. I know all about you." They began to tell me what had happened to me at different ages of my life. They shared how the traumas I experienced had affected me emotionally, how Jesus felt about these events and how He felt toward me now. As they described His thoughts and emotions toward me, one specific picture began to break down my walls of self-hatred and shame.

One student shared a simple picture God had shown him. He said, "Shelley, I see you at the age of nine. You are dancing in a field before your heavenly Father, and He is delighting in you. Despite all of the things that were done to you and the innocence you feel was stolen from you, the Father sees you as a pure and innocent little girl dancing before her Father. I see the Father reaching down and holding you in His hand. You are like a beautiful, untouched flower. He protected you through it all, and you are untouched, pure, and beautiful before the Lord." I was undone not only by his words but also by the purity with which they were spoken. I wept before the Father that night. Through one small picture my heavenly Father began to write a new story on my heart. I knew all was not lost. I had a heavenly Father who did not consider me tainted or ruined. It was as if the little girl inside of me stepped toward the light, shook herself from the dust, and allowed Jesus to clothe her in beautiful garments like the ones spoken of in Isaiah 52. I began to believe that night what my soul knows full well now—that Jesus makes all things new. There is nothing His blood cannot wash. He died to make the darkest heart pure again, and I am His beloved and precious little girl.

As we continued in prayer, the girl who was sitting at my feet began to weep uncontrollably. At a few points I actually looked down at her and thought, "This girl needs some help herself." I had no idea what was really going on in her heart. After everyone else had prayed, the girl, with her eyes red and swollen, pulled herself up from the floor using the sleeve of my sweater. She put her head as close to mine as she could and stammered out the words, "It's just that… It's just that…" Then she broke into sobs again. She did this three times before she was finally able to get the words out.

By this point she had my full attention. I couldn't imagine what was going on in this girl I barely knew. "It's just that… It's just that… He loves you so much!" When she spoke this to me, I wasn't able to receive the full impact of her statement, but what happened in my heart and mind was no less significant. As I looked into her eyes, I was convinced that what she was feeling was real and that if she, a human being, could know God's love for me that deeply, then I would do whatever it took to experience that reality for myself. I realized for the first time in my life that there is a God and that He loves me, and through the girl's witness I believed that love actually could be felt.

I was willing to do whatever it took to feel that love for myself. For the first time in my life I saw something powerful enough to heal the depths of pain I had been carrying through life. God had answered my second question from the psychiatric hospital by revealing His love for me. Yes, He could do something about the pain. His love was powerful enough to heal the wounds, and I would spend the rest of my life searching it out. By the grace of God, I am happy to say I am still searching it out even as I write these words.

My professor led me in a prayer for salvation, and I remember him telling me about the power of the Holy Spirit. He said, "Shelley, it is through the Holy Spirit that these students have spoken these things over you tonight. He is the One who gives them joy and peace. Jesus talked about the Holy Spirit being in you forever. Through the new birth He is in you. In the Scriptures, there is a fullness or baptism of the Holy Spirit that believers experience for sanctification, transformation, and empowerment. This is how the Holy Spirit is able to penetrate your mind, will, and emotions and propel you forward…"

He didn't even finish his sentence before I interrupted him and said, "Yes, yes, I want that! I can have God's joy in me forever? The Holy Spirit can work in my emotions, thoughts, and will? Then yes, I need the power of the Holy Spirit." As the precious group of believers gathered around me and prayed for me to be baptized in the Holy Spirit, I remember experiencing a massive shift in my heart and understanding of God. It was as if the Holy Spirit launched an all-out invasion upon all my faculties, filling me with His peace, love, and joy. A single tear rolled down my smiling face as I felt true joy for the first time in my life. I never knew how that felt before.

A New Life

When I arrived home that night, I could not put my Bible down. All of a sudden the Word of God was living and active in me, and I couldn't stop reading it and marveling over what I read. I cut up a huge pile of CDs that had been feeding my depression for years, and I began telling everyone around me about Jesus. I couldn't help myself. I arrived at every class early and asked if I could testify about what God had done in my life. Heads were turning as people whispered, "Is that Shelley Hundley? What happened to her?" I had gone from death to life.

After hearing my account of what had happened, my counselor, Lesley, gave me a huge hug and, weeping with joy, she told me she had been praying for me all along. She explained how she had experienced the power of the Holy Spirit in her own life and couldn't wait to see all that God would do in and through me. In the months that followed, Lesley told me again and again how overwhelmed she was with the speedy change God began to work in me. After one counseling session I remember Lesley saying, "Well, I have to tell you, Shelley, I am not your counselor anymore. Jesus is."

Our counseling sessions basically turned into testimony meetings. I would tell her what Jesus had been doing in me, and she would listen with joy and confirm His deep work. Lesley told me years later that what totally stunned her was that I went through every stage of the healing process. I didn't skip over anything; I just moved through every phase at warp speed. What takes years for most people took weeks for me, and what takes most people months took moments for me. Lesley said during those early days of God's work in my life that one day I would write a book and that through my story God would give hope to others who have suffered through sexual abuse and severe depression. They would know they can receive total healing and restoration by the power of His Spirit.

Lesley didn't live to see the fulfillment of her prophecy. She is with the Lord today, but I know she is smiling with the precious and tender gaze that Jesus used to impact my life so deeply. In some way, I'm sure she is saying, "I knew it, Shelley. I knew it."

Chapter Five

DISCOVERING THE LOVE OF GOD

A FTER WALKING WITH Jesus for only a couple of months, I was desperate for an opportunity to share all that He had done. I had shared my testimony in my classes, but I wanted to tell anyone who would listen about what had happened to me. Three times a week our college held required chapel services. Once a year each class was allowed to sponsor a chapel service and was responsible for choosing students to give testimonies, sing, and even preach.

The chapel service my sophomore class was scheduled to host was approaching, and our class president asked me if I would share my testimony. He had no idea what had happened to me, but many students on campus could see the drastic change in me and wanted to hear my story. I told him I would be happy to share, thinking, "Wow! What an opportunity to see God touch others the way He ministered to me."

Several testimonies were scheduled for that day, and I asked the class president if I could be the last person to share. He thought I was nervous. That was true, but that was not my reason for wanting to be last. I didn't exactly know how to do an altar call, but I purposed in my heart to do everything I could to see other students touched by the power of the Holy

Spirit as I had been. I believed that God would move even if I didn't have much biblical understanding yet.

When the day of the class chapel arrived, I was pretty nervous. Many of the other testimonies given that day were about seeing the majesty of God in creation, an experience at sunrise during summer camp, or some other neat reflection on the greatness of God. I knew my story was going to be very different from those. When I walked up to the podium, my opening lines were, "How would you like to a run race with your eyes blindfolded, legs shackled together, and your arms tied behind your back? That is what it's like to try to live the Christian life without the power of the Holy Spirit." I went on to share how far I had been from believing in Jesus, much less grasping God's love for me. You could hear a pin drop in that chapel as I said, "Many of you within the sound of my voice have been sexually abused as I have."

I told them I'd never learned about the Holy Spirit's power and His ability to meet us right where we are and pour His love into our hearts. I didn't have all the theological terms down, but I shared in my own words what had happened to me. I ended by saying, "There is no reason why any of you should leave this place today without receiving the power of the Holy Spirit in your lives."

Not knowing how to lead an altar call, I slipped out of my chair as the closing hymn was being sung and knelt at the wooden altar, hoping others would do the same. I wanted God to touch them as He had touched me. I will never forget the sound of the wooden altar rumbling as students poured to the front, kneeling before the Lord in tears. I stayed in the chapel for a couple of hours praying with people, not knowing fully how to release what I had received. But as students wept before the Lord, I knew He was visiting us.

Sitting in the back row of the chapel that day was a man named Allen Hood. He had attended Mike Bickle's church in Kansas City and was now a student at the seminary across the street. Allen came that day because someone he knew was also participating in the chapel. As he sat and listened to my testimony, he heard the professors around him say, "Is this Shelley Hundley?" God touched his heart, and he and his wife, Rachel, invited me to join their small discipleship group. The first day I attended a Bible study with Allen, he turned to John 17:24–26, grinned at the group of five or six of us with a bright sparkle in his eyes and said, "Today, I am going to tell you why you exist." That was the first time I heard the message that Jesus is our heavenly Bridegroom, who desires one thing from us: voluntary love. With an open heart, I believed and received every word of his teaching that day, and my journey into the love of God began.

A Divine Invitation

John 17 records Jesus's last prayer before He went to the Garden of Gethsemane, where He cried out to God before His crucifixion. We don't have to ask what Jesus was feeling before He was crushed for us. His desire is laid out clearly in John. He opens up His heart and lets us listen in on the most intimate moments of His life on earth.

> Father, I desire that they also whom You gave Me may
> be with Me where I am, that they may behold My glory
> which You have given Me; for You loved Me before the
> foundation of the world. O righteous Father! The world
> has not known You, but I have known You; and these
> have known that You sent Me. And I have declared
> to them Your name, and will declare it, that the love
> with which you have loved Me may be in them, and I
> in them.
>
> —JOHN 17:24–26

These phrases contain the very reason for which you were created and present an invitation to know God intimately—to really know Him and be near His heart. In His first request to His Father, Jesus asks to be near the ones He is about to purchase with His blood. He does not want us simply to be technically His; He wants us to be wholly His. The bride in Song of Solomon longs for this same intimacy. She says, "Why should I be as one who veils herself by the flocks of your companions?" (Song of Sol. 1:7). In her poetic language, the bride is essentially saying: "Jesus, I don't want my eyes to be covered. I don't want to be blinded from seeing You. I want to see You as You really are. Jesus, being near Your friends is not good enough! I want to be near You and to truly know You intimately in my own heart."

We long to be close to God because He first longed to be near to us. He is not a God who wanted to redeem us then stand at a distance. Rather He purchased us with royal blood so that He could put His own Spirit in us and spend now and eternity unveiling His heart to us.

In His second request, Jesus asks that we would see His glory. This is exactly the desire echoed by the bride in Song of Solomon when she said she did not want to be veiled from seeing the Bridegroom. Our heart cries, "Take away the veil, God!" Jesus's heart also cries out, "Father, I *desire!*" Can you imagine how heaven must have shaken when the God-man spoke that phrase in the garden that night? Can you imagine Him interceding for you right now asking the same thing?

Beloved, that is exactly what Jesus is doing right at this moment. The writer of Hebrews says that Jesus ever lives to make intercession for us before the Father as our faithful high priest (Heb. 7:25). In this very moment, Jesus is speaking to the Father, who loves you with the same love He lavishes on His Son—He is asking that the glory of who He is would be revealed to your heart.

Jesus's third request in John 17:26 is the greatest of all— that we would love Him. But let's look carefully at this. What kind of love does Jesus want from us? Does He want us to love Him as a grateful servant loves a benevolent master? No. Does He want us to love Him with whatever we can muster up after surviving a painful past? No. Beloved, when Jesus asked His Father that you and I would love Him, He reached for the greatest measuring rod He could possibly pull out— the amount of love the Father has for His only Son.

When I consider this truth, I always think of little children. Have you ever seen a child spread out his arms, stretching them as wide as he can, to show his parents how much he loves them? Or how about a kid who goes crazy with analogies? "I love you from here to the moon and back, and around the earth a gazillion times!" Jesus reached out as far as He possibly could, beloved, and in doing so He ended any notion that Christianity would be boring or that you and I could allow our pasts or family backgrounds to keep us from loving Him and being transformed into His likeness.

I know this language may seem awkward, but Jesus pulled out His Trinitarian checkbook and wrote you the biggest check He could. He put the whole account at your disposal. What Jesus did is sort of like a father who explains to his son that Father's Day is coming up. He then takes the boy to the store, helps him pick something out, and hands the child his credit card to pay for the item. At home the father helps the boy wrap the gift, and when the big day comes, the father helps his child pull the gift down from the closet shelf. When the boy hands over the gift, the father still lights up with joy, exclaiming, "I can't believe you got this for me. It's just what I wanted!"

Beloved, it really is that good. Jesus ends His prayer in John 17 by saying that the Holy Spirit's job description will be to take the love Father God has for His Son and put it in us. This way Christ Himself will be formed in us, and we can love God with the supernatural love He gives us. The kind of love Jesus is talking about here is eternal and unquenchable. It is a torrent of desire, a raging fire of light and exhilaration. Truly, out of the heart of the one who believes in Jesus will flow rivers of living water (John 7:38). God longs to release a river of pleasure inside you and me. It is a river of fire and of love that is waiting to be released in our hearts.

When we come to know Jesus and receive the Holy Spirit,

a river begins to flow in us, a river that has one desired end. The Holy Spirit in us longs to take us into the depths of God to remove the veil from our eyes and to help us see the glorious riches of the man Christ Jesus, converting even the most hostile heart into a torrent of holy affection for God. Do you have this vision for your life? Oh, my friend, if you are bored, I dare to say that it is your own fault. If you have quit trying to grow in love or have waited for "someday" to take on this pursuit, I beckon you back in to the journey.

Nothing about Jesus and what He has done for us is boring, and nothing in your past, present, or future can exclude you from knowing the love of Christ. He desires that you allow His waves and billows of affection to crash over you, leading you to new heights of love and compelling you to let your light shine before men. We read in Psalm 36:7–9:

> How precious is Your lovingkindness, O God! Therefore the children of men put their trust under the shadow of Your wings. They are abundantly satisfied with the fullness of Your house, and You give them drink from the river of Your pleasures. For with You is the fountain of life; in Your light we see light.

The Godhead has been in a perfect state of delight, pouring Their love upon One another. You and I exist because the Father created us to join in this holy fellowship. Yes, we are the creation and He alone the Creator, yet He has chosen to share His very life with us. The Godhead in perfect communion—without restraint or anything to make that love impure or diluted—has always been and always will be supreme happiness and delight. This is the love from which every other real love draws its potency. This is love undiluted and unpolluted—God loving God through God. From the Father to the Son to the Spirit, back and forth, love just keeps pouring out and pouring out.

In the middle of that desire, in the middle of that torrent of love, came a thought about you and me. In the midst of God's perfect fellowship of love, God thought, "This is too good. How can We not share this?" That is why you and I were created. The Bible says in 1 Corinthians 1:9, "God is faithful, by whom you were called into the fellowship of His Son, Jesus Christ our Lord." In John 14:23, Jesus says, "If anyone loves Me, he will keep My word; and My Father will love him, and We will come to him and make Our home with him."

What is my family history? Love. What is my background? Love. What is my destination? Love. The enemy's version of my existence was that I was abused, depressed, and headed nowhere. Yet somehow in the core of my being that story line never seemed to explain the reason for my existence. When I learned the truth that I come from Love, was an idea of love, and was created to love, I ran with it. I sat there as an eighteen-year-old in Allen Hood's Bible study, believing with all my heart that, yes, this is why I was created.

Reflecting on that time now, I can say with my whole heart that I believe this truth even more today than I did all those years ago. And can I tell you a secret? I am the happiest person I know! I pray you set your heart to pursue His love every day of your life. Jesus already wrote the check for you. He wants you to cash it in and give Him the gift He paid such a high price for—you.

A Recipe for Knowing God

I spent the summer after I came to know Jesus in the discipleship group Allen and Rachel Hood led with some other church leaders in the area. We spent several weeks preparing in prayer and Bible study, then went out as a team ministering in youth groups across the nation, predominantly in Methodist settings. I gained a lot of practice sharing my testimony and saw hundreds come to the saving knowledge of Christ. God also began to teach me about spiritual gifts as I struggled to figure out how to walk out life in the Spirit.

We also visited several places that were experiencing revival. At the Pensacola Outpouring in Florida, I was water baptized, and God filled me with the joy of the Holy Spirit. Because of this, I was able to get off all my antidepressant medication with no recurring bouts of depression. We also visited Kansas City, where Mike Bickle was pastoring a local church. During that trip, God spoke very clearly to my heart that I needed to attend his ministry school in Kansas City to grow in my understanding of God's love and to learn about the prophetic calling. From the first day I came to Christ and was filled with the Holy Spirit, God had been giving me prophetic revelation, though I didn't fully understand it at the time.

In Kansas City, God used Mike's teachings on the love of God to touch my heart in a deep way, and I began to dive into the Word. Everything I read only left me more and more confident that God wanted to give me an even deeper revelation of His love. In this season of discovering God's love, I learned a principle that changed my life completely when I truly grabbed hold of it. Mike explained that we are all created to love and know God. No one is excluded from the deep transformation He wants to bring through this pursuit. But many people make knowing God difficult when it is actually very simple. Mike gave us this easy-to-remember "recipe": mind, mouth, heart:

1. Mind

First, we must fill our minds with new truths about what God is like by meditating on the love of God and the deep emotions God feels for the ones He loves. This includes listening to teachings and reading books on the subject, but that is not enough. We must study God's Word to fill our minds with new information and allow God to rewrite the code in our hearts, so to speak. (See John 16:13; Romans 12:2.)

2. Mouth

Filling our mind with new truths is not the end of the story. We must then take those truths and speak them back to God in prayer. This means that our prayers must change from bargaining with God or simply telling Him how we feel to actually declaring His truth. For instance, "Jesus, I thank You that You love me. You asked the Father that I would be with You where You are, that I would see Your glory, and that I would love You. So come now and fill my heart with Your love. I receive Your truth into my heart today, and I ask You for fresh revelation of who You are."

Proverbs 18:21 says, "Death and life are in the power of the tongue, and those who love it will eat its fruit." We can't just think about wanting to change or plead with God to change us. We must fill our minds with new truths about what God is like and speak those truths before the Lord. We also have to change the way we talk to others. After all, the most influential voice we will ever hear is our own. I found that it was good for me to share how I felt with others, but it was even more impacting when I chose to speak the truth about who God is even when I didn't feel it yet.

3. Heart

I remember Mike saying, "If you fill your mind with the knowledge of who God is and then actually speak it in prayer, it will touch your emotions. It's God's promise to us that if we do our part, He will do His." I hung on to this truth even when many people told me that though I was saved, there were limits to how much of God's love I could know. Armed with verses such as Romans 5:5—"Now hope does not disappoint, because the love of God has been poured out in our hearts by the Holy Spirit who was given to us"—I filled my mind with new truth from the Word of God. As I spoke the Word in prayer and in my conversations with others, I began to grow in my understanding of the love of God. I actually began to feel God's love and be empowered to love Him back. When I began fasting regularly, I found the process was expedited greatly. We don't fast because we can earn anything from God; we fast precisely because God already loves us, and we want to get more in touch with that reality.

Discovering the Bridegroom

Sitting under Mike's teachings, I heard many messages about understanding God's love for us that presented Jesus as the Bridegroom and the church as the bride of Christ. John the Baptist spoke of this very revelation when a group of people asked how he felt when Jesus was baptizing more people than he was. He said, "He who has the bride is the bridegroom; but the friend of the bridegroom, who stands and hears him, rejoices greatly because of the bridegroom's voice. Therefore this joy of mine is fulfilled" (John 3:29). We hear the voice of Jesus our Bridegroom in His Gethsemane prayer as He expresses His desire for those who would be with Him and love Him.

Understanding our identity as the bride of Christ is not a gender issue. John the Baptist lived a rough lifestyle out in the wild desert and ultimately was decapitated for challenging the highest-profile leader of his day, King Herod. Yet when asked about baptizing, the very thing he was best known for, John showed no hint of jealousy toward the One whose ministry was greater than his own. Instead, John said he received his joy from knowing Jesus as the Bridegroom.

In his relationship with God, John knew he was a part of Jesus's bride. In his relationship to others through his ministry assignment, John understood that he was a "friend of the Bridegroom," which in our day would be called the "best man." It was John's great joy to see Jesus the Bridegroom's heart revealed to others and to be sure he did not distract the bride from her true Bridegroom. This was the secret to

John the Baptist's identity and the joy that kept him faithful to His mission.

I find it amazing that John the Baptist received this revelation so clearly from the Lord and was able to see past the outward appearance of the man from Nazareth who was in fact unmarried. John was not only able to see Jesus as the promised Messiah, but he also was able to see the deepest motivations of His heart and mission. Jesus was a Bridegroom looking for a bride, and He still is.

The language John used in this passage is also very important. John doesn't say Jesus is like a bridegroom or that He occasionally acts like one in order to motivate us to serve or love Him more faithfully. John says, "He who has the bride *is* the bridegroom" (John 3:29, emphasis added). He knew the secret that Isaiah foretold (Isa. 62:5), that Hosea declared (Hosea 2:19), and that the apostle Paul would later call a great mystery (Eph. 5:25–32). Jesus also used this language when He identified Himself as the Bridegroom in Matthew 9:15. He referred to His own disciples as "friends of the bridegroom" and made longing for Jesus as the Bridegroom the motivation behind all the sacrifices and spiritual disciplines we would embrace as Christians.

The Book of Revelation tells us that before Jesus returns, the church will understand her identity primarily as "the bride." More than "the army" or "the servants," the Holy Spirit uses "the bride" to describe the church at the return of Christ (Rev. 21:2, 9; 22:17). Of all the books in the Bible, the Song of Solomon paints a vivid portrait of Jesus's love for His bride. Throughout church history, this book has been understood primarily as a love story about God and His people, and secondarily for its wisdom about marital relationships.

This was an extremely difficult concept for me to understand when I first took Mike Bickle's class on the Song of Solomon in 1996. I had been studying John 17, but I still was struggling with seeing Jesus as our Bridegroom. Yet as I continued to study, I found this picture of Jesus as our Bridegroom throughout the Word of God. A light bulb began to turn on in my mind and heart when I began to realize that, yes, this truly is how God feels about you and me. This truth is not sensual in any way. Sensuality never enters into our relationship with Jesus; rather, the Bible uses the language of Bridegroom and bride to reveal our position as those who are cherished and loved by the Lord. Understanding Jesus as our Bridegroom gives us insight into how the transcendent and holy God deeply loves and cherishes us and desires to share His full authority and resources with us as His bride.

When confronted with this picture of Jesus in my class on the Song of Solomon, I felt everything inside me rise up to resist this undeserved love that I kept hearing about week after week. At times I even found myself physically grabbing the chair, just to keep myself from running out of the class. This truth was hard for me to take. I felt like each class was the same message, repeated like a broken record: He loves you. He loves you. He loves you.

The very words the group of students prayed over me the night I accepted Christ and was baptized in the Holy Spirit were being pounded into my heart through this study of God's Word. I remember the night in Mike's class when I reluctantly participated in the altar call and surrendered to this truth. I said in essence, "OK, Jesus. If You are determined to love me with this overwhelming, cherishing love, and Your heart is truly ravished over me because that's who You are and how You see me, then fine. Go ahead and love me. I give up."

To this day, I am sure Mike Bickle still smiles when he thinks of me standing at the front of the class with my arms folded and a scowl on my face, waiting to receive prayer. The recipe Mike taught us for knowing God—mind, mouth, and heart—worked for me in the end, and it will work for all those who give themselves to prayerful meditation on God's Word.

Over the next two years, I grew in my understanding of Jesus's love. I became one of the most joyful people I knew, but there was still an area in my heart that had not yet been addressed. Deep inside was a longing for justice that I didn't know what to do with. No matter how many times I tried to simply let go of the past, something in me just couldn't let it go.

Chapter Six

WE NEED A JUDGE

O NE DAY DURING a time of prayer, the Lord whispered a phrase to me that opened up an entirely new revelation of Jesus. I had no idea at the time, but the truth the Holy Spirit was about to reveal would bring me more healing than I could have possibly imagined. I was meditating on the Song of Solomon and preparing my heart to receive more of God's love. I whispered a prayer asking the Father for a fresh revelation of the beauty of Jesus when suddenly I heard a statement that was so clear and unexpected, it startled me. The words were, "You need a judge."

To be honest, I thought it was the enemy trying to get me back into the old, abusive paradigm, where I felt God hated me and was constantly judging me. I rebuked the thought in the name of Jesus and tried to focus again on expressing my heart to the Lord and receiving more of His love. I wish I could have seen the Holy Spirit's gracious smile as I rebuked the revelation He was trying to give me. Praise the Lord that, as my good friend Allen Hood loves to say, the Holy Spirit only came to one man as a gentle dove; to the rest of us He comes as an all-consuming fire we can't shake off.

Undeterred by my dismissal, the Holy Spirit spoke again, this time with a tenderness I could not mistake. He said,

"Shelley, you don't know how much more you will love Jesus when you know Him as your Judge. Shelley, you need a Judge!"

This time God had my attention. Though the statement still seemed strange to me, I couldn't deny that the Holy Spirit was trying to lead me into a new revelation of Jesus as Judge. I knew the principle of taking biblical truths, thanking God for them, and turning them into prayers. So I rather sheepishly and awkwardly whispered back to the Holy Spirit, "I need to know Jesus as Judge. I need a Judge." The words felt strange, and I had no idea where this was going. But I stuck with it and kept praying, "Holy Spirit, I need a Judge. Holy Spirit, show me the places in my heart where I need a Judge."

This time I felt something. It wasn't an overwhelming revelation that invaded my entire being in one moment, but I began to feel something rising up within me. It was a cry for justice that I didn't realize I had suppressed in my attempt to be godly. As I began to feel some deep emotions rise within me, I panicked a bit, thinking, "God, I hope You know what You're doing!" Have you ever had God put His finger on a wound so deep that, with all of your might, you just hope He will be able to finish whatever He is starting? Although we know in our minds that He who began a good work in us is faithful to complete it (Phil. 1:6), moments like this often feel as though we are diving into a chasm of pain we may not escape alive.

That is how I felt when the Holy Spirit began to bring up the issue of justice, yet I knew I needed to stay on this course no matter how difficult and painful it seemed. I followed the trail of this revelation in the Word of God. As I began to study out the biblical theme of God as Judge, the prophet's vision of Jesus in Isaiah 63 captured my heart. In this passage, the prophet Isaiah cries out, "Who is this," because the vision of Jesus is so different from the one recorded in Isaiah 53. In that earlier chapter, Jesus has "no beauty that we should desire Him" and is "despised and rejected by men, a Man of sorrows and acquainted with grief" (Isa. 53:2–3). Yet in Isaiah 63, He is "glorious in His apparel, traveling in the greatness of His strength" (Isa. 63:1).

In its literal interpretation, this passage depicts an event that will take place in the future. The Bible tells us that Jesus will come marching through the land surrounding Israel in a marvelous procession when He returns and brings this current age to a dramatic end. He is seen in Isaiah 63 striding from Edom (modern-day Jordan) and Bozrah (its ancient capital), through the nations that have opposed and oppressed His people, and bringing forth justice and deliverance.

This literal picture of Jesus the Judge has massive implications for each of us who is dealing with his own areas of oppression and injustice. The appearance of Jesus is glorious. He is seen here in the power stride of all power strides. Think of a majestic lion with total domination in his eyes advancing toward his prey. Or a king decked out in splendor, His full resources behind Him at every step, indicating his complete commitment and determination.

This description of the Second Coming procession of Jesus is what Israel expected to see at His first coming. Instead, He baffled the minds and offended the hearts of Israel when He came into the city riding on a donkey. They expected a great warrior, but Jesus made no attempt to overturn the oppressive Roman regime even when they threatened His own life.

Have you considered the reality that Jesus came once on a donkey but will come very differently when He returns as the righteous Judge and ruler of the whole earth? Beloved, we must recognize Him as a fierce Judge, for this is how He will come when He returns. It is this Jesus in Revelation 6:14 whom kings and great men flee from, climbing under rocks and hiding in caves.

Robed in Judgment

This picture of Jesus the Judge was so surprising to Isaiah that he asked, "Who is this?" Jesus answered, "I who speak in righteousness, mighty to save" (Isa. 63:1). In essence, He is saying, "I who said I would deliver you am here now to back it up with indisputable action."

Jesus is determined to end sin. He is committed to finally put an end to the pain and suffering we inflict upon one another in this world. And most of all, He wants to end mankind's utter rejection of God and all that He calls good. Isaiah 42:4 says, "He will not fail nor be discouraged, till He has established justice in the earth; and the coastlands shall wait for His law."

Do you know this Jesus? Has the Holy Spirit truly imprinted upon the depths of your soul the image of a God who is faithful and not only speaks but also acts on your behalf as the mighty Judge? We must feed on this revelation until it lives in us. Consider the picture of Jesus painted in Isaiah 63:2–3:

Why is Your apparel red, and Your garments like one who treads in the winepress? "I have trodden the winepress alone, and from the peoples no one was with Me. For I have trodden them in My anger, and trampled them in My fury; their blood is sprinkled upon My garments, and I have stained all My robes."

Here we see an image of Jesus as the only one worthy to release the fierce judgment of God. He drank the cup of His Father's wrath in Gethsemane (Matt. 26:42) so that now He is the only one worthy to pour it out. (See Revelation 5:1–10.) In this role as Judge, Jesus is not just drinking a cup of wrath; He is meting out the judgment Himself, dispensing the perfect measure of righteous and just judgment upon the wicked.

The passage in Isaiah 63 uses the phrase "their blood." It is not the blood of Jesus that has spattered His robes. Jesus is covered in the blood of His enemies. The imagery of the winepress is consistent in the Bible to depict a just God giving the wicked their due, the fruit of sin that will now set their teeth on edge. (See Joel 3.) The red of the wine also refers directly to blood. Those who reject the Father's gift of His Son are depicted as having "trampled the Son of God underfoot" (Heb. 10:29).

Those who think they have the upper hand on Jesus and reject God's free gift of salvation because they consider themselves above it will in the end find themselves trampled underfoot by a fierce God. He will not allow sin to corrupt or harm His people again in the age to come. The Bible indicates in Isaiah 40:27 that in the last generation before the

Lord returns, many will believe that God does not see or hear and will not take an account of sin.

Jesus's statement in Isaiah 63:3 that His activity as Judge has "stained all My robes" speaks of the fact that in the generation when the Lord returns, all of His actions will be in the context of global judgment and shaking. Throughout Scripture, robes refer to our deeds and actions.

Jesus is also speaking to His bride, saying in essence, "If you are looking for Me to put something else on because you are uncomfortable with my activity as Judge, then know this, I have nothing else to wear! This is who I am, and this is what I will display in an unprecedented way before I return." If we are to love Jesus, we must love Him in this aspect of His activity as Judge. This is how our Bridegroom dresses, especially as the day of His return draws near.

Jesus also wears these "robes of judgment" at His return. In Revelation 19 we read: "Blessed are those who are called to the marriage supper of the Lamb!...Now I saw heaven opened, and behold, a white horse. And He who sat on him was called Faithful and True, and in righteousness He judges and makes war. His eyes were like a flame of fire, and...He was clothed with a robe dipped in blood" (Rev. 19:9, 11–13).

God's strategic, temporal judgments (such as those listed in the Book of Revelation) are His final knocks on humanity's door. He wants to let us know that we are failing the test and are completely wrong to think that He has not taken notice of sin or does not care what we do to one another. He cares deeply about how we respond to His gift of mercy and His provision for transformation and holiness of heart.

Through His righteous judgments, He actually teaches us what He truly cares about. His small judgments prepare us for His all-encompassing eternal judgments. (See Isaiah 26:8-9.) They are humanity's final invitation to turn to God before the moment when eternal judgment comes upon us and we have no more time to repent.

As God's shakings increase in the earth before His return, the Bible gives us some understanding about how the church will respond. Initially, many people will be confused and angry as they struggle to interpret God's activity as Judge. This will be a completely new paradigm for them (see Matthew 11:6), but the Holy Spirit has promised to grant the church insight as we renew our understanding through the Word (Jer. 23:18–20). The Book of Revelation tells us that in the end the church will understand and glorify God in the midst of His judgments. (See Revelation 19:2.)

A Day of Vengeance

Isaiah's vision continues as Jesus answers his question, "Why is Your apparel red, and Your garments like one who treads in the winepress?" (Isa. 63:2). Why such a fierce response to sin, Jesus? Why such a terrifying display of irreversible judgment and wrath? We are led in this moment to ask what motivates this part of God's nature and activity. Is Jesus meting out judgment because He is capricious and angry? Does He enjoy crushing the weak and seeing people die? Jesus offers a stunning answer. He says that the "day of vengeance" is in His heart, and He links that fearsome time of judgment and vindication with the "year of My redeemed" (Isa. 63:4).

What is He saying here? There is a day Jesus is dreaming of and waiting for—the final day of vengeance when He brings sin to its end and secures the well-being of everyone who turns to Him. There are also lesser days of vengeance in which Jesus releases His justice upon sickness, oppression, sin, and persecution. Releasing healing, deliverance, and breakthrough in the area of holiness and the ability to overcome in the midst of adversity and persecution are in a sense acts of God's righteous vengeance upon the evil one.

Jesus's vengeance works in mysterious ways, and we are reminded in Scripture that only He is qualified to dispense wrath in perfect righteousness. It is His to do, not ours to figure out, but there is a deeper truth in this revelation. There is a day of vengeance in the heart of Jesus for you. If we search out the phrase "day of vengeance," we find it used in several other passages of Scripture. (See Isaiah 34:8–10, 61:1–3; 63:4; Proverbs 6:34–35; Jeremiah 46:10; Luke 21:22.) In Isaiah 34:8–10, the phrase is used in the context of the final judgment upon sin and "recompense for the cause of Zion." In Isaiah 61, the day of vengeance is tied to Jesus's ministry of comfort to those who mourn:

> The Spirit of the Lord GOD is upon Me, because the LORD has anointed Me to preach good tidings to the poor; He has sent Me to heal the brokenhearted, to proclaim liberty to the captives, and the opening of the prison to those who are bound; to proclaim the acceptable year of the LORD, and the day of vengeance of our God; to comfort all who mourn, to console those who mourn in Zion, to give them beauty for ashes, the oil

of joy for mourning, the garment of praise for the spirit of heaviness; that they may be called trees of righteousness, the planting of the LORD, that He may be glorified.

—ISAIAH 61:1–3

The apostle Paul picks up this theme in 1 Thessalonians 4 when he asks the church to comfort one another with the knowledge of the coming Judge. The passage in Isaiah 61 also shows that the day of vengeance is part of the good news to the poor and healing for the brokenhearted. This is a rich truth that we will examine more fully in the coming chapters.

Of all the references to the day of vengeance, the most pertinent to Isaiah 63:4 may be in Proverbs 6:34–35. This passage reveals a significant insight into the motivation behind the day of vengeance. It says, "For jealousy is a husband's fury; therefore he will not spare in the day of vengeance. He will accept no recompense, nor will he be appeased though you give many gifts."

Here we see the precise reason the day of vengeance is in God's heart. He is a Judge because He is a Bridegroom. The terrifying vengeance He displays comes from the jealous heart of a Bridegroom who says, "This is *my* bride. How dare you touch her?" Jesus's fierce actions come from the heart of a Bridegroom who intends to remove all that hinders love or tries to make a prostitute out of His bride.

I looked, but there was no one to help, and I wondered that there was no one to uphold; therefore My own arm brought salvation for Me; and My own fury,

> it sustained Me. I have trodden down the peoples in
> My anger, made them drunk in My fury, and brought
> down their strength to the earth.
>
> —ISAIAH 63:5–6

No one else is worthy to bring forth God's final judgment upon sin and deliver the righteous. (See Revelation 5:1–10.) The Father's standards are high when it comes to who will stand as the Judge of all humanity. His generous heart goes far beyond what we deserve. God desires to put a Judge before us who no one can say is unsympathetic. This judge must be fully man, tempted and tested as we have been, yet uncorrupted by absolute power. He must use His authority to lift the weak rather than to crush them. Jesus is this righteous Judge, as Isaiah 42:3 says, "A bruised reed he will not break, and a faintly burning wick he will not quench; he will faithfully bring forth justice" (ESV).

As the perfect Judge for humanity, Jesus will not be indiscriminant with His judgment, accidentally bringing wrath or losing His temper. Even in the most terrifying images of judgment, Jesus does not fly into a rage and use His power to crush the weak out of spite. He sees the struggling believer who cries out to Him as a "bruised reed" that He will not break. He does not stop being merciful in order to bring forth justice. He does not suspend one attribute to express another. He judges righteously and justly and is perfectly merciful and kind every step of the way.

In Isaiah 63, the Lord makes a profound statement by following the terrifying vision of the Judge in verses 1-6 by then painting one of the most tender and beautiful pictures of God's love for His people in verses 7-9:

> I will mention the lovingkindnesses of the LORD and the praises of the LORD, according to all that the LORD has bestowed on us, and the great goodness toward the house of Israel, which He has bestowed on them according to His mercies, according to the multitude of His lovingkindnesses. For He said, "Surely they are My people, children who will not lie." So He became their Savior. In all their affliction He was afflicted, and the Angel of His Presence saved them; in His love and in His pity He redeemed them; and He bore them and carried them all the days of old.
>
> —ISAIAH 63:7–9

The Holy Spirit is making a point to us that everything we saw in the preceding verses depicting Jesus in His fierceness is 100 percent consistent with the God who is love itself. In fact, it is because of His great love that He fights fiercely against everything that keeps His people from experiencing His love.

As I uncovered some of the hidden gems in Isaiah 63, I began to simply pray the passage back to God phrase by phrase, putting myself in the story line. At the time, my prayer closet was an unfinished basement. I still remember pacing back and forth, speaking this passage out loud in kind of a dramatic way to get these truths written on my heart. I would shout out, "Who is this who will fight for Shelley?" Then I would answer myself from the Lord's perspective saying, "It is

I, the Lord, who speaks in righteousness, mighty to save! The day of vengeance is in My heart for you, Shelley!"

It may sound humorous, but the Lord began to touch my heart in a deep way during those prayer times. After each of those encounters with the Lord, I emerged out of the basement understanding more and more about the heart of Jesus the Judge. I wholeheartedly invite you to do the same. You can come to Him now in prayer:

> *Jesus, I want to know You as my Judge. Heal the broken and wounded places in my heart by revealing Yourself to me as the One who fights for me and will avenge the wrong done. Thank You, Lord, for hearing my cry and knowing my sorrow. You love justice and will not forsake Your beloved ones. You are mighty to save, and the day of vengeance is in Your heart. You are a jealous Bridegroom who fights for His bride. Let this truth transform my heart and mind, and bring me more comfort, peace, and joy than I ever imagined possible. Thank You, Lord, for being my Deliverer and my soon coming King. In Jesus's name. Amen.*

Allow the Holy Spirit to continue His work in your heart by praying the truth of the Word back to God, seeing yourself as the one Jesus fights for. These are just two of the powerful verses that can be used for personal meditation:

For the LORD loves justice, and does not forsake His saints; they are preserved forever, but the descendants of the wicked shall be cut off.

—PSALM 37:28

And the LORD said: "I have surely seen the oppression of My people who are in Egypt, and have heard their cry because of their taskmasters, for I know their sorrows. So I have come down to deliver them."

—EXODUS 3:7–8

Only when we have come to know Jesus as the Judge will we have adequate answers for the most broken people we encounter each day, people who are crying out for justice yet who do not know the One to whom they can direct their cry.

Chapter Seven

THE JUDGE FIGHTS FOR US

As we saw earlier, John 3:29 is one of the most descriptive verses about Jesus in the entire Word of God. John the Baptist tells us, "He who has the bride is the bridegroom." The Bible does not simply say that Jesus is *like* a bridegroom but rather that in every part of His being, the Bridegroom is who He is. Every motivation of the heart of Jesus comes from His heart as the Bridegroom.

Contrary to what some believe, the illustration of the bride and Bridegroom in Scripture isn't borrowed from the earthly relationship between husbands and wives. It is the opposite. Earthly marriages exist because Jesus is a Bridegroom and loves His bride. He is the example of love that Ephesians 5 calls husbands and wives to model. What we experience with our spouses in the natural is meant to point us to Jesus, our heavenly Bridegroom.

Jesus's great love for His bride compels Him to act on her behalf. His judgment is borne from a heart that is ravished by His bride, the church. God's fierce vengeance and the Bridegroom's love for His bride are intricately connected. Proverbs 6:34–35 speaks of a husband who has caught someone forcing His wife to commit adultery: "For jealousy is a husband's fury; therefore he will not spare in the day of vengeance. He will accept no recompense, nor will he be appeased though you give many gifts."

In this passage, the Bible says the husband will act with jealous zeal or He is no husband after all. He will not take a bribe or be deterred when it comes to protecting His bride. The idea of God's judgment being motivated by love may seem contradictory, but this modern-day parable may help illustrate this concept.

Imagine a couple who is deeply in love. Early one evening, the wife leaves home to pick something up from the grocery store. When she doesn't return after several hours, the husband begins to worry. Then the phone suddenly rings. The local police are on the line and explain to the frantic husband that his wife has been assaulted. She was brutally beaten and violated in the dark parking lot of the supermarket.

The officer tells the husband that his wife is in the hospital in stable condition, but her body is badly bruised, her clothes are torn, and she is in a state of emotional shock. The husband races to the hospital, not even noticing the traffic signs as he hurries to reach his wife. When he walks in he is directed to the bed where his wife is receiving medical attention.

The husband takes his wife's hand and begins to wipe the tears from her eyes, embodying the epitome of tender love. He speaks to her in hushed tones, saying, "I love you. Honey, I am here. You are OK now. We'll get through this. You're so beautiful to me. I love you." He weeps, kissing her tenderly and stroking her hand, his heart breaking with tender love for her. He wants her to feel safe, cherished, and loved. The husband continues to whisper to her, "Just rest, my love. It's OK. I'm here."

Now imagine that the doctor walks in, gives the husband the medical report on his wife's injuries, then casually says, "By the way, the man who attacked your wife is standing across the hall. He's over there drinking a soda. The police didn't feel the need to take him in or press charges."

What happens to the heart of a true bridegroom as he hears this? If he is indeed this woman's husband and he loves her, his tender love will take on a very different expression. The husband's gaze will meet the eyes of the man who attacked his beloved, and his fury will be evident. The police had better arrive soon because there won't be enough money in the world to dissuade the husband from dealing with the man who harmed his wife without consequence.

This is exactly what Proverbs 6:34 is describing. If the husband didn't act to protect his wife and had no interest in dealing with her attacker, restoring her honor, and ensuring that she is not harmed again, he simply would not be a true husband. The Word of God is filled with moments when Jesus the Bridegroom responds with the very same zeal. In the Book of Revelation the most terrifying judgments are poured out upon an evil system that is shedding the blood of the church, Jesus's bride. (See Revelation 19:1–2, 11–12.)

God's judgments have been misunderstood as the acts of a capricious god who gets in a bad mood one day and lets humanity have it. In actuality His actions can best be interpreted as those of a loving Bridegroom who erupts with judgment upon wickedness as His heart cries out, "You harmed

My bride. You touched her. You did not take into account that she is Mine. Answer to Me then!" Jesus the Bridegroom fights against sin, sickness, and demonic oppression on our behalf. We can take our case to Him, and He will fight for us.

Holy Fear

Having quite a bit of experience teaching young people here in Kansas City at the International House of Prayer University and in other nations, I am convinced that this generation needs more faith for personal holiness than for the miraculous demonstrations of God's power. Many of the students I teach are struggling with sin, and they don't know whether God can truly set them free. They don't realize that this is exactly what the Judge wants to do.

God is not only our Bridegroom but is also our Father. To view God as a Father who doesn't fight for His children is to see Him as a weak parent who puts food on the table but won't lift a finger to protect his family from harm. This is not a picture of our Lord. He protects His children from hurt, whether we inflict harm on ourselves or it comes from outside oppressors.

The Bible says the judgments God released upon ancient Egypt came from the heart of the Father wanting to protect His children. (See Exodus 4:22.) Because Pharaoh refused to free Israel, God's firstborn son, God struck dead Egypt's firstborn sons. Just as God delivered Israel from bondage in Egypt, so will He free us from the strongholds of sin that seem to overwhelm us. (See Deuteronomy 1:30–31.) As the righteous Judge, our heavenly Father not only loves us with tender affection but also will fight to set us free from the bondage of sin when we step into agreement with Him.

Young people who never had clear boundaries or a father to protect them and who saw love as nothing more than selfish lust will impose these views on their paradigm of God. Instead of truly understanding God's love, they will merely transpose their moral ambiguity about love onto their view of God. Unless they come to understand the jealous side of God's love, they will be left with an anemic view of Jesus. They'll come to view Him as a boyfriend who is kind of interested in them but doesn't think they are worth fighting for. The results of this wrong thinking are catastrophic.

When my students share with me issues of sin they are dealing with, I will often say, "Let's take it to the Judge." If they have committed the sin, they are typically fearful and nervous, and my response always surprises them. I ask, "Do you hate the sin and want it out of your life? If you do, then the Judge is the greatest ally and advocate you could have. He knows how to remove this from your life."

The reality is that if we hate the sins we are still in bondage to, then the Judge is our greatest friend. He will fight to set us free, and He will release the spirit of the fear of the Lord, which has the power to turn our hearts away from sin. The evil one wants to try to get us to back away in shame. The enemy knows how powerful it will be if we grasp the reality that Jesus the Judge is for us and not against us.

Jesus has given us all authority over demonic influence in our lives, and He has called us to partner with Him in helping others find freedom. Perhaps this is why deliverance is one of my favorite areas of ministry. I love to see Jesus render judgment upon the demonic forces that have ravaged lives. Praise God that as the righteous Judge, Jesus has the victory and releases freedom to His people.

I love the delivering power of Jesus displayed in the story of the demon-possessed man from Gadarenes in Mark 5. The demon asked Jesus if He had come to torment him before the appointed time. In some ways, Jesus's answer was yes as He expelled the demon. Of course, we should not go around tormenting demons. That is absolutely not advisable. But we cast them out in the name of Jesus, and this example of the demoniac is a foretaste of the judgment they will receive when Jesus throws every demon into the lake of fire along with Satan himself.

The Judge releases holiness through the fear of the Lord. We were created to fear something, and if we do not fear God, we will fear everything but God. If our view of God does not include trembling before His majesty and holiness, then we are not worshiping the God of the Bible. (See Proverbs 2:1–5.) For the revelation of Jesus as our Bridegroom to be accurate and the mercies of the Father to be rightly interpreted, we must have a revelation of the fear of the Lord.

The fear of the Lord can be understood as lovesick trembling before a mighty and holy God. It is the knowledge that He sees all and that we will give an account to Him. The fear of the Lord beckons us to remember that God is watching moment by moment and second by second, and that He sees when no one else does and will truly take an account.

Therefore the fear of the Lord cannot be understood outside the context of God as Judge.

The fear of the Lord keeps us from comparing ourselves to the people around us. It lifts our eyes to a higher standard that all human beings must be judged by, the very nature of who God is. He is holy (Isa. 57:15). God is beckoning us in the midst of a crooked and perverse generation to set ourselves apart as holy unto the Lord. If the prophet Daniel was able to remain holy in the heart of Babylon, a city known for its wickedness and idolatry, then, beloved, the same God can empower you and me to walk in holiness as well. (See Daniel 4:8, 9; 5:11.)

Because of the calling on his life to preach radical holiness, John the Baptist was filled with the Holy Spirit in his mother's womb (Luke 1:15). Later in his ministry, John spoke of the coming baptism in the Bridegroom's jealous fire.

> I [John the Baptist] indeed baptize you with water unto repentance, but He [Jesus] who is coming after me is mightier than I, whose sandals I am not worthy to carry. He will baptize you with the Holy Spirit and fire. His winnowing fan is in His hand, and He will thoroughly clean out His threshing floor, and gather His wheat into the barn; but He will burn up the chaff with unquenchable fire.
>
> —MATTHEW 3:11–12

John the Baptist was speaking of the coming Holy Spirit, whose job description included the commission to "sanctify you completely" (1 Thess. 5:23). This is a job the Holy Spirit loves to do! If you and I submit to His work, He will give us clean hearts and minds, purifying us both inside and out.

The baptism of the Holy Spirit empowers and sanctifies us spirit, soul, and body. He is perfecting us in love so we can be presented to Jesus as His blameless bride. Rather than allowing us to be ruled by the lusts of our flesh (body) or the brokenness of our emotions and thinking (soul), the Holy Spirit is being released as a mighty champion within us, winning us for Jesus.

As we are transformed more and more, the Holy Spirit gains ground, reigning in every region of our being. There is no greater miracle than a human being who manifests Christ in every ounce of his being! Oh, to be free to become what we dream of—radical lovers of Jesus Christ, a bride worthy of Him!

We grow in the fear of the Lord as we tremble before a holy God and cooperate with the sanctifying work of the Holy Spirit. We want to grow in this grace and be able to respond in reverential fear as Jesus's coming draws nearer and His judgments are displayed more and more in the earth (Ps. 9:16; Rev. 15:2–5). Let's take a closer look at the definition and benefits of the fear of the Lord.

1. The fear of the Lord raises our standards from the earthly to the eternal. A holy reverence of God removes any illusion that the Lord will not take an account of sin or that He can be bargained with or bribed (2 Chron. 19:6–8, Isa. 11:3; Ps. 19:9).

2. The fear of the Lord makes us wise. It lifts us from earthly to heavenly wisdom and actually escorts us into the knowledge of God (Prov. 9:9–11, Job 28:28, Isa. 11:2; Jer. 9:24).

3. The fear of the Lord is an eternal reality. The Bible says in Psalm 19:9, "The fear of the LORD is clean, enduring forever."

4. The fear of the Lord breaks the stronghold of sin in our lives and empowers us for holiness. According to Proverbs 8:13, to fear the Lord is to hate evil.

5. The fear of the Lord removes all lesser fears from our lives. Holy fear shows us how big God is and how small our own issues are in comparison. The fear of the Lord will propel us into righteousness as we see the One whom we truly should fear (Ps. 86:11; Isa. 52:13, 8:12–14; Matt. 10:27–29; 1 John 4:18).

The Jealous Bridegroom

During the prophet Jeremiah's day, God was preparing to unleash horrific judgment upon the southern kingdom of Israel. As He was about to release His wrath, the first words He asked Jeremiah to speak on His behalf were these: "I remember you, the kindness of your youth, the love of your betrothal, when you went after me in the wilderness, in a land not sown" (Jer. 2:2–3).

In the midst of one of the greatest hours of judgment in Israel's history, when God allowed a wicked army from Babylon to demolish both Jerusalem and the temple, burning everything to the ground and slaughtering the people, God was filled with loving nostalgia. He wanted to weep and reminisce about the love His people used to show Him. He said through the prophet, "Can a virgin forget her ornaments, or a bride her attire? Yet my people have forgotten Me days without number" (Jer. 2:32).

God is using poetic language to convey the attitude of His heart: the moment of His judgment is also the time when He misses His people the most. His heart aches with longing as He says, "Have I been a wilderness to Israel, or a land of darkness? Why do My people say, 'We are lords; we will come no more to You?'" (Jer. 2:31). It's impossible to miss the tone here. The almighty God sounds like a betrayed lover; His hurt is much like that of an earthly husband whose wife has cheated on him. God essentially asks, "Why did she have to leave Me to get something from someone else?"

As believers, we are no longer objects of God's wrath, but we are objects of His jealous love. He shakes us to remove the distractions that hinder our love and in the process reveals the duplicity in our hearts toward Him. The reality that Jesus is our Bridegroom is the best and worst news for humanity. It means we are loved and cherished beyond measure, but it also means that Jesus demands *all* of our hearts and will not share us with another.

As our Bridegroom Judge, He tenderly disciplines us so we can be more fully His. (See Romans 5:8–9, Hosea 2:1–20, Haggai 2:6–7; Hebrews 12:7–11.) Think of a Father who wrestles a knife out of a toddler's hand or holds his child down while the doctor gives him a shot. The Lord shakes us from areas of compromise to empower us to love Him more completely, and we should praise Him for it!

What's more, the Bridegroom delays judgment because of His love. Our Lord could judge all of humanity and snuff out every wrongdoer, but He chooses not to because of His great love. Second Peter 3:7–8 says God preserves the heavens and the earth until the Day of Judgment. He is long-suffering because He wishes that none would perish. So not only are His judgments released for love, but His restraint also is due to love. The heart of the Judge truly is the heart of a Bridegroom!

Chapter Eight

THE JUDGE BRINGS US COMFORT

W HEN I WAS battling through depression and suicide, the greatest comfort others seemed to have for me was that somehow I would continue to exist. The only hope they could give me was that the traumas I endured would slowly lose their power and stay in the locked room I was trying to create for them. Never in my wildest dreams did I think the pain I was experiencing would ever end.

I was told to look for the light at the end of the tunnel because "things would get better." In the darkest moments of my journey, pats on the back and teary-eyed sympathy brought little consolation. This may be part of comforting others, but it is in no way the full message of comfort the Bible reveals. Scripture declares that Christ came to "comfort all who mourn" (Isa. 61:2), and Jesus reiterated that promise in His Sermon on the Mount (Matt. 5:4).

True Christianity offers the world extraordinary hope, but too few believers know this. Tainted by our humanistic culture, modern Christianity seems to have taken on powerless strategies for bringing hope that are no different for the believer than for the unbeliever. Without recognizing Jesus Christ as the ultimate Judge, the comfort we offer those withering under the weight of a wicked and perverse world is reduced to offering them a sympathetic pat on the back and the shallow encouragement, "You will make it through somehow."

Without the revelation of God as Judge, we have no real response to the darkness and torment human beings are bringing upon other human beings. We end up no better off than our neighbors who do not have even a glimpse of the coming hope and see no end to the tragedies in their lives. Eventually we retreat from witnessing of Jesus to a world that actually has us stumped, as we cower under the age-old question of why there is suffering and injustice in the world.

We are ashamed to proclaim that God is a Judge. We hide this truth like a drunken uncle whose unseemly and unpredictable behavior embarrasses us during the annual family reunion. Meanwhile we are oblivious to how bankrupt our faith and witness have become without a living knowledge of God as Judge. Influenced by a relativistic culture, we have backed historic Christian theology on judgment into a corner, where this "inconvenient" message is no longer mentioned in our witness or as part of our experience of the gospel.

This aspect of God's character and personality makes us wary because we don't want to be seen as bigoted and judgmental or to present God as such. Yet in the process of taming the gospel, we have lost one of the most needed benefits of Jesus as our Judge. Scripture reveals that the entire message of comfort hinges on the statement, "Take comfort, the Judge is coming!" Consider the apostle Paul's words to the suffering and persecuted believers in Thessalonica:

For the Lord Himself will descend from heaven with a shout, with the voice of an archangel, and with the trumpet of God. And the dead in Christ will rise first. Then we who are alive and remain shall be caught up together with them in the clouds to meet the Lord in the air. And thus we shall always be with the Lord. Therefore comfort one another with these words.
—1 Thessalonians 4:16–18

To give you who are troubled rest with us when the Lord Jesus is revealed from heaven with His mighty angels, in flaming fire taking vengeance on those who do not know God, and on those who do not obey the gospel of our Lord Jesus Christ. These shall be punished with everlasting destruction from the presence of the Lord and from the glory of His power, when He comes, in that Day, to be glorified in His saints and to be admired among all those who believe, because our testimony among you was believed.
—2 Thessalonians 1:7–10

This is such a radical departure from our current definition of comfort. The apostle Paul comforted the Thessalonian believers with one truth: the Judge is coming! When God comforts those who are being persecuted, He calls them to look forward to His coming as the day when His people will be fully restored and delivered.

Comforted in Persecution

In the Book of Revelation, God comforts those who are being martyred in the Great Tribulation. The martyrs ask God to avenge their blood, and He says in essence, "Wait a little longer, and I will." He doesn't give them a shallow promise of light at the end of the tunnel, nor does He limit His response to tears and empathy. Instead He gets them to focus forward, looking to the day when He will ultimately make all the wrong things right (Rev. 6:9–11).

Revelation is in essence a manual for martyrdom. Jesus's recipe for enduring persecution and death is to remind us that the Judge is coming. He tells us clearly how He will bring all of it to an end and take an account for the shed blood of His people. This concept may be more difficult for Western Christians to grasp because we have not known this level of suffering for righteousness' sake and therefore have not needed this level of comfort.

In nations where anti-Christian persecution is common, the Book of Revelation comes alive among the underground church as believers look forward to the coming of Jesus, who will bring them comfort through His judgment. Growing up in the midst of Colombia's death culture, I saw a true picture of persecution and martyrdom. This is precisely the type of setting in which the message of taking comfort in Christ's return is most potent.

Wrapped up in a bloody civil war that began in 1964 and is still going on today, Colombia has been notorious for Christian persecution, murder, and kidnapping. When I was growing up there, young boys worked as hired assassins with the same frequency and ease American kids took on paper routes for extra money. Sometimes I wish I could take back some of the curiosity I possessed as a kid. Too often I looked in the wrong direction at the wrong time. Some of the things I saw defy description.

After my family moved into one particularly difficult neighborhood in Bogotá, my brothers and I made a pact not to tell one another about the horrible things we saw. This was not unusual. Missionary kids in dangerous and persecuted countries often observe a code of silence. You just didn't discuss how bad things were with anyone. The feeling was, your parents are already making sacrifices to live in a difficult environment, so it is better not to make them feel any worse or more stressed about the situation. Plus, many missionary kids fear being sent to boarding school. We heard terrible things about these schools, but those claims were spread mostly by other missionary kids who were making the schools seem much worse than they actually were.

This code of silence meant we kids were on our own to survive. We would tell one another or the adults only when a situation got too far over our heads. No doubt this code also contributed to my silence about the sexual abuse I experienced. Colombia's violent culture was one thing, but the strategic killing and kidnapping of Christians was a whole other layer in the nation's tapestry of terror. At that time, guerrillas regularly entered churches with machine guns and told everyone to line up on one side or the other. Those who would renounce their faith went to one side, and those who refused were sent to the other. The people who did renounce their faith were made to watch as the guerrillas gunned down those who refused to deny Jesus.

I remember one night a man burst into our house just as

we were finishing dinner. He had been in a church when the guerrillas came in, and, paralyzed with fear, he had renounced his faith and watched as members of his own family were killed. Another time, troops stormed onto the seminary campus, and I had to grab the little kids and hide under a bed, covering their mouths. The guerrillas would steal the national army's uniforms so we could never tell who were official troops and who were rebels. Ultimately it made little difference because of the corruption that was commonplace.

Either group might kill or kidnap you, which made troops of any kind bad news. As I was hiding several small children under the bed, I heard my dad walk out to talk to the leader of the troops. My dad's Spanish was absolutely perfect, and sometimes people mistook him for a bodyguard. Lying under the bed, with my hand covering the younger children's mouths, I wondered if this would be the last time I would hear my father's voice. Yet somehow he convinced the commander of that troop that he had the wrong address, and all the soldiers left.

The guerrillas specifically targeted our family multiple times. Most of the Americans were leaving, and I remember at one point our Colombian friends and staff from the seminary were actually angry with us for returning to Colombia after our planned furlough. When we arrived at the airport in Colombia, our friends were in tears, and everyone was silent. They knew our family was in great danger because we had been targeted by the guerrillas. My parents did a phenomenal job of talking with my brothers and me about the threats made against our family, and they allowed us to be part of deciding whether or not we would return to Colombia. We were very young, but all of us were willing to die for Christ because we saw this as a great privilege. *"Pues si vivimos,"* one of the popular hymns in the churches we attended, captured the dire situation believers in Colombia faced during those years and still today. It says whether we live or die, we belong to the Lord. This song was sung in the most difficult times—when people came to church to see who was still alive.

Our small school for missionary kids was tucked inside a coffee plantation so it would be hidden from aerial bombers. Every day when our driver took my brothers and me to school, he had to perform all kinds of crazy stunts in order to lose the guerrillas following us. It was almost a game to us.

Later on, when we were attending a different school in Bogotá, I remember a fellow schoolmate being called out of class because her father had been kidnapped. In those cases, we typically didn't even get to say good-bye before the family was evacuated. We usually never saw that person again. Another fellow missionary kid was kidnapped, then mysteriously released. We never learned what happened to her. She simply disappeared, then reappeared without explanation.

God's Message of Comfort

It is in these types of environments that we long for the day of Jesus's appearing, when He will come to judge and bring an end to sin and death. Whether we are speaking to Christians experiencing the level of persecution that exists in Colombia or simply encouraging a fellow believer facing common trials, we must understand what the Bible says about comfort so we are equipped to release this message to the suffering. The premier chapter on the message of comfort is Isaiah 40, which opens with the words, "'Comfort, yes, comfort My people!' says your God."

The repetition of the word comfort reflects how important this message is to God and for His bride. He promises to come "with a strong hand" and to feed His flock like a shepherd. Isaiah 40:11 says He will "gather the lambs with His arm, and carry them in His bosom, and gently lead those who are with young."

This picture of comfort is God's promise to a people who feel hidden from the Lord and passed over by Him (Isa. 40:27). The pain of their suffering pierces God's heart, and He reminds them of His power to bring rest and strength to those who will lift up their eyes and behold the comfort of the coming Judge.

> Have you not known? Have you not heard? The everlasting God, the LORD, the Creator of the ends of the earth, neither faints nor is weary. His understanding is unsearchable. He gives power to the weak, and to those who have no might He increases strength. Even the youths shall faint and be weary, and the young men shall utterly fall, but those who wait on the LORD shall renew their strength; they shall mount up with wings like eagles, they shall run and not be weary, they shall walk and not faint.
>
> —ISAIAH 40:28–31

The whole chapter is saturated with references to the sovereignty of God as He seeks to lift the chin of the sufferer, beckoning us to "lift up our eyes" and "behold our God." The revelation in this chapter is so rich, it deserves a closer look. These are some of the essential proclamations presented in Isaiah 40:

1. Behold your God (Isa. 40:9). God calls us to lift our eyes from our current circumstances and look to Him. The persecution and suffering we face has a way of capturing our full attention, leaving our hearts prone to discouragement and causing us to forget who Jesus really is and what He is like. While we are experiencing pain, the evil one is always present, accusing God in our hearts. Therefore the message of comfort must lift the eyes of the sufferer and cause us to "behold our God."

2. God shall come (Isa. 40:10). God's promise to the sufferer is sure: Jesus is coming! The New Testament church focused their hearts upon Jesus's return. This wasn't because they had an escapist attitude, which we sometimes see in the church today, but because the promise of His coming shaped their hope and daily attitude before the Lord. When we truly learn to look for the "day of His appearing," we will find our hearts steadied in suffering and

sharpened in holiness. This message is needed today in a climate that constantly assumes things will remain as they are. Many believe that history will simply cycle around and around in sin, with brokenness as its only constant. Biblical truth shouts at us saying, "No! Do not be deceived; He shall come!"

3. With a strong hand (Isa. 40:10). Jesus is not simply coming; He is coming with a strong hand. This phrase indicates that He is willing and able to deliver His people. Our Bridegroom is not weak; He does not grow weary. He is coming with a strong hand of deliverance. This revelation adds urgency to our witness to the lost as we realize that the Lord truly will come and take an account of the wrongs done to the saints. Jesus came the first time as a baby in the manger, but He will come the second time in flaming fire, taking vengeance and judging all sin and oppression.

4. His arm shall rule for Him (Isa. 40:10). Throughout Scripture, Jesus is called the "arm of the Lord." This phrase speaks of the strength with which God reaches out and brings forth into real time and space the zeal for righteousness and justice within His heart. In this verse of Isaiah 40, the sufferer is promised a righteous

King who will come and establish justice as
He rules and reigns forever in the coming age.
The world's injustices, suffering, and pain will
not continue forever. In this phrase lies God's
pronouncement that He has a perfect plan for
humanity. Jesus will be our King and our Judge.

5. His reward is with Him (Isa. 40:10). In times of
   suffering it is easy to feel that there is no sig-
   nificance in our suffering. Here God speaks to
   the heart of the sufferer, reminding us that the
   same God who comes with a "strong hand" to
   remove oppression will also come with reward
   for those who have loved Him and suffered for
   Him. This phrase from Isaiah 40 is God's declaration that the attitude of our hearts matters in
   the midst of trial and suffering. Jesus does not
   only take note of the negative things that occur
   on the earth, but He also sees all the movements of our hearts toward Him and rewards
   us openly for how we carry our hearts in secret.

6. His work is before Him (Isa. 40:10). Before Jesus
   returns, His work already will have begun to
   break forth. He will shake the earth and release
   the strategic judgments listed in Revelation,
   which will begin to shatter the evil systems
   present in the world. The purpose of these temporal judgments is to check wickedness in the

earth and to serve as the final knock on the hearts of the world's inhabitants. Christ's work of judgment precedes His final return at the end of this age, and these shakings are warnings that His eternal judgment is near.

7. He will feed His flock, gather the lambs with His arm, carry them in His bosom, and gently lead (Isa. 40:11). This verse shows us that Jesus will be fierce to the enemies of His bride. Yet He will carry His people with tender love in the midst of His wrath against their oppressors. There are two sides of the love of Jesus: (1) His tender love for His people, and (2) His fierce commitment to remove all that has hindered intimacy. There is no contradiction between these two realities.

Although we may feel we are under the grip of fierce persecution, we can have comfort knowing our God will come and fight for us, bringing swift judgment upon the evil one while carrying us in His bosom like little lambs.

I invite you to study these themes more fully because their truth is truly transformative. Below are several key themes about God's comfort that you can meditate on and study:

1. God's comfort strengthens us.

The Latin word for *comfort, confortare*, means "to strengthen" or "to increase fortitude." This is the outcome we experience when we truly understand God's message of comfort.

They shall see the glory of the LORD, the excellency of our God. Strengthen the weak hands, and make firm the feeble knees. Say to those who are fearful-hearted, "Be strong, do not fear! Behold, your God will come with vengeance, with the recompense of God; He will come and save you."

—ISAIAH 35:2–4

The message of comfort cries out, "Strengthen the feeble knees and weak hands. Strengthen them in the midst of the suffering they are enduring. Strengthen them to overcome." It is not just a gentle and compassionate consolation but also a real and effectual strengthening.

2. God reveals Himself as the comforter.

Comfort is actually part of God's nature and one of the terms used to describe the Holy Spirit (John 14:16, 26; 15:26; 16:7, KJV). God repeatedly says in Scripture that He will comfort His people (Isa. 51:3; 66:13; Zech. 1:17; 2 Cor. 1:3–4; Acts 9:31).

3. Scripture describes prophecy as a type of comfort.

The Bible says whoever prophesies speaks edification and comfort (1 Cor. 14:3). The Word of God also points to the comforting hope of Christ's second coming (Rom. 15:4).

4. The comfort we receive becomes a comfort to others.

The Word of God gives us a mandate to proclaim comfort to those who suffer. Jesus said in Luke 22:32, "But I have prayed for you, that your faith should not fail; and when you have returned to Me, strengthen your brethren." (See also 2 Corinthians 1:3–4; 7:13.)

5. God's comfort draws people back to Christ.

The Holy Spirit works upon the hearts of those who have sinned, empowering them to repent of their sin and compromise, and return to God. Second Corinthians 2:6-7 says, "This punishment which was inflicted by the majority is sufficient for such a man, so that, on the contrary, you ought rather to forgive and comfort him, lest perhaps such a one be swallowed up with too much sorrow."

As one of the names of the Holy Spirit, as the defining characteristic of prophecy, as an aspect of God's nature, and as a central component of the gospel, comfort is so much more than an attempt to make someone in pain feel better. It is a key component of the gospel and one of the major tools God uses to strengthen His body. This is why it is so important that we pursue a biblical understanding of comfort.

Receive God's Comfort

Comfort seems most elusive when we are in the midst of our own suffering. The promises we read in Scripture can seem like empty words when our hearts are racked with pain and there seems to be no end in sight. When we are in the midst of our suffering, we must lift up our eyes and receive comfort by seeing who Jesus truly is.

> 1. *See Jesus as your Bridegroom.* He is longing for you and weeping with you. As your heavenly Bridegroom, Jesus endured the pain of the cross for the joy of having you. By His grace you can endure pain for love of Him because He has

endured pain for love of you. See yourself as the cherished bride of the all-powerful Bridegroom, and let that become the center of your identity. Your wedding day is soon to come.

2. *See Jesus as the Judge.* Jesus is the Bridegroom Judge who will fight for you. Commit your cause to Him and demand that every bit of pain bear fruit. Let it draw you into deeper intimacy with the Bridegroom Judge and equip you for His purposes.

3. *See God as your Father.* The Father records the movements of your heart toward Him. That is how deeply He cares for you. God uses the least amount of suffering possible to equip you for what He has for you. Surrender to His wisdom and sovereignty when you don't understand.

4. *See God as your Deliverer.* We don't have to choose between intimacy and deliverance. We can hold both in their glorious paradox. We can say yes to God in the midst of our pain (by cultivating intimacy with our loving Bridegroom) and believe God for the deliverance He will bring as the righteous Judge. We must ask God to make our suffering count to the highest measure, believing God to bring healing and deliverance from all oppression.

I challenge you right now to open up your heart and allow God to bring you comfort. He promises to comfort all who mourn. I pray that you will be strengthened by the hope that the King is coming. No matter what you are facing, behold your God. He will come with a strong hand.

Chapter Nine

A BEAUTIFUL EXCHANGE

W HEN I CAME to know Jesus as my Savior and was filled with the Holy Spirit, I began to experience freedom in many areas of my life. But one area that didn't fall easily into line was my sense of self-worth. Although I knew Jesus loved me, I couldn't change the way I viewed myself. I remember living with a precious Christian family the first year after I came to know the Lord. During that time, they constantly challenged me to stop apologizing when there was no real need to do so.

If someone in the family asked me to pass the salt at dinner, my response would be, "I'm sorry. Here it is." I did this all the time. Whenever anyone addressed a comment to me, I apologized. Even my physical demeanor seemed cowering and apologetic. One day, the precious mother of the family sat me down and brought this to my attention. I had never realized it before, but when she brought my incessant apologizing into the light, I began to see that my real problem was deeper than misplaced contrition. I realized that I felt sorry about my very existence. Deep inside I still thought I caused the abuse I suffered, and I thought if something that big was my fault, then I must be to blame for these smaller problems as well.

In my own convoluted thinking, I felt I should have known to pass the salt before having to be asked. If any conflicts arose, I reasoned that somehow I was to blame. Generally speaking, I felt worthless or, worse, worthy of mistreatment and abuse. When I talked with counselors, most of them told me this was not uncommon and that I might struggle with it for the rest of my life. After all, how could I reprogram something I had internalized at such a deep level?

Still today, the current crop of self-esteem gurus can't reach the core of human beings who have been damaged at extremely deep levels. This leaves victims open to more hurt and woundedness that, sadly, is often self-inflicted. Many victims of sexual abuse feel such a lack of dignity and worth that they throw themselves into more immorality because they no longer think what is done to their bodies matters. The trauma can mark victims so deeply that even when the physical danger is over, the internal pain and feelings of shame and worthlessness can feel unbearable.

During one of my hospitalizations I wrote a poem that paints a vivid picture of the deep sense of shame I felt I could never escape:

> I know too well a wretched hell, where screams and
>   hands and darkness tell
> Of muffled rage that never fades, a girl so small,
>   innocence betrayed
> Surrendered her untrampled age
> Surrendered her untrampled age.

His mouth devoured like a beast that drools at the
    enormous feast
He crushed, consumed the little child, to him his
    dream to her defiled
And every childlike scream reviled
And every childlike scream reviled.

There is a thought that haunts her night, that lingers
    deep yet out of sight
The beast has gone, the beast remains, ever the girl is
    not the same.
Her wounds can't heal too deep the stain,
Will even death remove this shame?

More unbearable than the fears, terror, and nightmares was the ache inside that made me think I would never have dignity and worth again. I felt unrecoverable. Praise God, this has absolutely changed, and we will explore why throughout this chapter. I didn't realize it until years later, but my journey toward healing from shame and worthlessness began when the college students prayed over me that night in the basement of my history professor's house. I caught a glimpse of God's love in the eyes of the girl who said to me, "It's just that He loves you so much!"

After that experience, I was never able to resign myself to an existence defined by the wrongs committed against me. It would be several years before Jesus's light finally touched the deepest places of my heart and lifted my head in dignity, but the miracle that began during that prayer meeting launched me into a depth of freedom I never could have imagined.

Beauty for Ashes

One day I was having coffee with a friend, listening to her talk about the fresh revelation she had received in the Word about Jesus. She was a few steps ahead of me in her quest to know the Lord more intimately, and she was sharing truths I had not considered or yet studied in Scripture. I had recently been giving myself to prayer and fasting at a whole new level, but it seemed that more pain was coming up in my heart during these prayer times. I was constantly comparing myself to other Christians I knew, people like this friend who seemed to have much less baggage.

As she talked about the revelation that was stirring in her heart, I came to a crisis point. My mind groped for language for what I was feeling, but overcome with emotion I just burst into tears. Then I finally sputtered out, "I will never know God like you do! It's like we're on a race to know God, and everyone else is so far ahead of me. You are talking about understanding Jesus as your Bridegroom and King, and I keep getting sidelined because I can't even know the love of God as Father and trust that He is good. If I can't even get that, I will never be where you are!"

My friend cried with me and responded to my meltdown with words that would radically shift my relationship with God for years to come. She said, "Shelley, I will never know God's goodness like you do. You can't get up tomorrow morning if you don't believe God is real and that He is good. You can't breathe without that revelation. Your very life depends upon your understanding that God is good and that

He loves you. The pain you have experienced is like a hallway leading into rooms of revelation I will never be invited into. Are you kidding me? I will never know God the Father the way you do.

"Yes, I had a good background and was able to learn from godly leaders, and I have strong foundations God can use as building blocks to give me revelation of His heart. But I fast and enter into a place of solitude in prayer to try to uncover my own buried need for God as Father. If the search for the knowledge of God is like a train, you already have the ticket in your hand, but you're asking me for ten dollars so you can buy a ticket.

"Your pain is your escort into the knowledge of God. I have to work hard to come into contact with my own need. Your need is already there. All you have to do is take the escort of pain and direct it all toward God."

Her words left me dumbfounded. It seemed too good to be true, yet for some reason it resonated in my heart. I began to search the Scriptures concerning this topic, and what I found was truly life-changing. I saw God using an economy of pain to bring us to a place of transformation.

Pain is a great unifier; every human being has experienced it. The pain of loss, abuse, trauma, etc., all point back to the source of all pain—our need for God. The pain of a broken earthly father, a lack of love, or betrayal in marriage ultimately reveals our need to know Jesus as the heavenly Bridegroom who loves and cherishes us.

Viewing things this way began to shift the way I responded when pain surfaced in my heart. As someone who has been engaged in pastoral ministry for many years, I have seen again and again that as people enter into deeper intimacy with God through prayer and Bible study, more, not less, pain seems to surface in their hearts. This is exactly what was happening to me when my friend gave me such profound encouragement.

Although it's counterintuitive, I encourage people to view those new levels of pain as invitations to move deeper into the heart of God. The Father offers a great exchange in the midst of pain. He doesn't say, "Forget your ashes, get over it, and I will give you beauty." Rather as we give Him our ashes, He gives us His beauty to replace our pain (Isa. 61:3). The glory of what Jesus has done in my heart is not that I am "over it," but that room by room and pain by pain I have reached out to Him, and He has given me beauty for the pain. I want the outcome of my life to be that I took every invitation Jesus offered me and did not shrink back from encountering Him in my deepest hurt.

A few years ago I had the opportunity to revisit the home in Medellín where I experienced the most horrific abuse during my childhood. The house was vacant and looked exactly as it did when I was there as a young child. Yet as I walked through each room, I neither relived the trauma nor experienced the suffocating fear. Instead, I kept thinking, "Jesus and I made it through this. I am not alone in the grief of what happened in this room. Jesus has helped me through and transformed each pain into a place where He has met me. I have exchanged ashes for beauty in each of these rooms."

It is only in this level of partnership with Jesus, when we

allow Him into every hurt, that we will find the strength to take a generation by the hand and lead them through the greatest time of suffering the world will ever see. Tribulation is coming to the whole earth, and God is raising up forerunners who have learned to encounter Jesus in the midst of pain. He has trained them by fire so they can help others experience the great exchange God has for every suffering servant who reaches out to Him.

A Divine Trade

Let's look deeper into Isaiah 61 and the exchange God offers here and in many other portions of Scripture. Much of the church has been quick to say, "God is with you," but they have not been willing to add, "God is with you *to deliver you.*" Reminding people of Jesus's tears without acknowledging His power to act on our behalf presents an incomplete paradigm. When we refuse to allow room in our theology for the transformation God can work in the heart of the sufferer, we are underselling the redemptive power of the cross.

No one can outdo or overdo God's redemptive power to heal our deepest pain. Who among us can even attempt to put a cap on how much God can do in the hearts of those He purchased with royal blood? Can we ever say, "Well, the blood of Jesus can redeem this type of suffering but not that level"? Many people actually told me I would live with the feelings of shame and low self-worth forever. They said those were scars I would just have to carry and that I should be content that at least Jesus saved me and set me free from depression.

However, God kept filling my heart with a vision for

something more as I studied His Word. I found that the cross possesses infinite power to redeem. Jesus was crushed, spit on, and mocked. He took upon Himself every sin I committed, every sin committed against me, and the sins of all nations throughout every century. How could anyone consider that sacrifice and tell Jesus, "You are not enough for me"? How can we limit the power of Jesus's blood and say, "Yeah, but You can't transform my brokenness. My pain is too big. My wound is incurable." We cannot draw a line and say this is how far Christ's redemptive work will go in transforming a wounded heart.

The exchange of pain for beauty is not a figurative, poetic picture. It is a literal trade, a real transformation. In the economy of God we do not merely put Christ's redemptive work on top of our old wounds so those hurts don't show as much. No, the Lord works a much deeper transformation in us. He takes our ashes so we don't have to carry them anymore, and by His blood He gives us not ordinary beauty, but the beauty Jesus Christ Himself possesses. His righteousness becomes ours (2 Cor. 5:21). Because of what Jesus did on the cross, we become something new—the very righteousness of God. This is the divine exchange.

I remember the freedom I experienced when I realized that Jesus's blood was enough to make me clean again and restore the purity that was taken against my will. He gave me a clean heart, and I was able to move forward as a new creation in Christ, not a limping, never-ending project. The Lord changes our pain. He does not simply say, "Forget your hurts; just discard them." Our pain counts before God! He dignifies it and uses it as currency in a miraculous exchange—His beauty for our ashes, the oil of joy for mourning, the garment of praise for the spirit of heaviness (Isa. 61:3). This is a literal trade.

We see this exchange at work also in the comfort God brings to those who mourn. Matthew 5:3–4 tells us that the poor in spirit shall inherit the kingdom of heaven and those who mourn will be comforted. In this passage we see a direct link between receiving comfort and the state of mourning. It is as if the Lord is saying that His deep comfort will meet the degree of our mourning. The Greek word for *comfort* used in this verse is *parakaleo*, which shares the same root word used as a name for the Holy Spirit (Paraclete) in John 14:16 to describe the Holy Spirit's work as our Comforter.

The third Person of the Trinity comes alongside those who mourn and pours His comfort into the depths of their sorrow. God wants us to know that His exchange rate is extravagant; He will fill us with His comfort to the degree that we recognize our need for Him. The exchange God offers does not help those who refuse to give Him their pain, but the Bible promises that those who open their wounds before the Father will be comforted, and what they will receive from the Lord will be great.

> "Sing, O barren, you who have not borne! Break forth into singing, and cry aloud, you who have not labored with child! For more are the children of the desolate than the children of the married woman," says the LORD. "Enlarge the place of your tent, and let them stretch out the curtains of your dwellings; do not spare;

lengthen your cords, and strengthen your stakes. For you shall expand to the right and to the left, and your descendants will inherit the nations, and make the desolate cities inhabited."

—Isaiah 54:1–3

In this passage from Isaiah, God tells the barren woman to stretch out the curtains of her dwelling and lengthen her cords because she will need to make room for all the justice He is going to pour out on her. He is basically saying, "You are going to be so lavished upon, so well paid, that you need to find more space in which to put all the bounty I will pour out on you when I stretch out My hand on your behalf."

He also tells the barren woman that in her final condition she will have more children, more abundance, than the married woman who never came to Him because she thought she had it all. Somehow in the mystery of God, He will recompense those who appear to have the least. In the end, their abundance will far exceed that of those who never reached out to God because they thought themselves rich enough in circumstance and experience.

God's generosity does not stop here. When we come to Him with the currency of pain, He gives us *double* honor for it. For every measure of shame and pain we hand over to Him, He gives us double in honor and beauty. Isaiah 61:7 says, "Instead of your shame you shall have double honor, and instead of confusion they shall rejoice in their portion. Therefore in their land they shall possess double; everlasting joy shall be theirs."

The depth of the wound, twice multiplied, is the

recompense God offers those who reach out to Him when they long to draw back in shame. In His kindness, God has chosen the universal currency of pain and assigned it an extravagant exchange rate: double honor for shame. We do not have to perform or clean ourselves up in order to qualify. Whether our pain is small or great, if we give it to Him we will be rewarded far more than we can imagine. He will pay so well for the weak movement of our hearts toward Him that we will still be reaping His lavish benefits in the age to come (Eph. 2:6–7).

Please stop for a moment and ask the Holy Spirit to illuminate areas where Jesus may be extending this same invitation to you, asking you to open for Him. Ask the Holy Spirit to help you identify the rooms deep within your heart to which Jesus is gently seeking access. He wants to come in, heal, and restore you. You will emerge richer because you allowed Him in.

Vengeance Belongs to God

It is the knowledge and revelation of the beauty of God that beautifies us. One of the truths of Scripture that began to beautify and heal my heart at the very core was the knowledge that I was worth fighting for. As I studied Jesus the Judge in Isaiah 63 and several passages in Revelation, I was shocked to discover that God actually asks us to give Him our greatest wounds of injustice because He will fight *for* us. In hindsight, this makes perfect sense. How can our worth and dignity be restored if we are not worth fighting for?

Like many victims of abuse, I wasn't rescued from the abuse. No one was aware of what was happening to me, and no one made it stop. As an adult I confronted the person who wronged me, but the responses he gave were not helpful in any way. Those closest to me were struggling through their own pain over the situation, and I felt very alone. The lingering question remained, "Who will fight for me?" When we believe there is no justice and that no one will take an account for what happened to us, we feel an inherent sense of worthlessness. We think, "If no one cares about what happened to me, then I must not be worth much at all."

These feelings of worthlessness can affect even those who haven't experienced the trauma of abuse or other physical pain. The Bible says feelings of worthlessness can come on the people of God when they are not rightly taught that God takes an account for wrongs. In Jeremiah 23, the Lord urges His people not to listen to the destructive teaching that says those who despise the Lord and do wrong will somehow be blessed and have peace.

> Thus says the LORD of hosts: "Do not listen to the words of the prophets who prophesy to you. They make you worthless; they speak a vision of their own heart, not from the mouth of the LORD. They continually say to those who despise Me, 'The LORD has said, "You shall have peace"'; and to everyone who walks according to the dictates of his own heart, they say, 'No evil shall come upon you.'"
> —JEREMIAH 23:16–17

This is exactly what our culture screams at us every day. We are taught in subtle ways through the media we watch and hear and in not so subtle ways in the schools we attend that there is no clear right and wrong, and certainly no God who takes an account. Although it may seek to do the opposite, this philosophy actually undermines the value of human beings. How can we settle the issue of our worth when there is no God to fight for the oppressed and no judgment to right wrongs?

We should have long ago given up hope that a government or other system will bring justice to wrongdoers. No matter which political candidate is elected, the injustices continue. As a result, we consider ourselves and others worthless, and as a society we degrade human life. We are in a hole that we dug and cannot get out of, and the last thought in our minds is that we need a Judge.

For a time in my own life, I couldn't find my worth or stop apologizing and cowering no matter how much I tried to pull myself up by my bootstraps. The fact that no one was ever punished in the natural for the horrible violence committed against me, coupled with the loneliness I felt as an adult as I faced the effects of the abuse, made me think that on my own I could not overcome. I believed there was no one who cared enough to fight for Shelley Hundley and that I would have to live with the shame and feelings of worthlessness forever.

But as I reached out to God in my pain, devouring His Word and spending hours in prayer, truth began to sink into my heart. I saw in Scripture a God who fights for me, and God began to rewrite the negative story line that had been etched on my heart through so much pain. Suddenly what I was reading in the Bible and praying back to God became more real than the lifelong suffering the enemy kept throwing at me. I began to look forward. I began to hope. I began to feel cherished. I began to believe.

I can't overstate the role God's Word played in this miraculous transformation. I meditated on His Word hour after hour, believing that if I drew near to Him, He would draw near to me (James 4:8). If the transformation I've been describing seems impossible to you, I encourage you to study and pray through the Scriptures as I did. These passages were particularly helpful to me on my journey:

> Say to those who are fearful-hearted, "Be strong, do not fear! Behold, your God will come with vengeance, with the recompense of God; He will come and save you."
>
> —Isaiah 35:4

> For the day of vengeance is in My heart, and the year of My redeemed has come.
>
> —Isaiah 63:4

> So truth fails, and he who departs from evil makes himself a prey. Then the LORD saw it, and it displeased Him that there was no justice. He saw that there was no man, and wondered that there was no intercessor; therefore His own arm brought salvation for Him; and His own righteousness, it sustained Him. For He put on righteousness as a breastplate, and a helmet of salvation on His head; He put on the garments of vengeance for clothing, and was clad with zeal as a cloak. According to their deeds, accordingly He will repay, fury to His adversaries, recompense to His enemies; the coastlands He will fully repay.
>
> —Isaiah 59:15–18

Pacing back and forth to keep myself alert during my long prayer times in the basement of the house where I lived, I pored over these verses, and they began to come alive in my heart. I began to picture Jesus with eyes of flaming fire, His jealous gaze fixed on me, and crying out, "Someone will pay! Someone must pay for what was done to Shelley, and I will take an account. I will never forget Shelley."

God began to reveal His jealous fury to me, and I felt the intensity of Christ's commitment to take an account for the abuse I experienced. The fierceness of His anger was terrifying as I read these passages and felt the presence of a real and present Judge who would fight for me.

At first, I wanted to say, "Jesus, it's not that big of a deal. I mean...I am OK. It's history at this point." Even though I wanted to know who would fight for Shelley Hundley, I was terrified by the Lord's answer. It forced me to confront the deep issues of worthlessness in my heart. No one had ever responded to my abuse with that kind of righteous anger.

It was all so new and so fierce that I honestly did not know how to respond as Jesus revealed His fury to my heart. Yet as I spent hours in prayer, I realized that I could do nothing to make Jesus back down from His jealous love and commitment to fight for me. The Scriptures made it clear that vengeance belongs to God (Deut. 32:35–36; Ps. 94:1–3; Jer. 51:6; Nah. 1:2–3). I could not ask Him to be less than who He is, and I had no right to minimize His response to the gravity of what was done to me.

No matter where I looked in the Scriptures, I seemed to run into the same truths. Every word seemed to penetrate my heart more, and I reached my breaking point. I could no longer resist the fiery gaze of the One who called me precious in His eyes and saw in me someone worth fighting for. He seemed to impress the words of Isaiah 43 upon my heart:

> But now, thus says the LORD, who created you, O Jacob, and He who formed you, O Israel: "Fear not, for I have redeemed you; I have called you by your name; you are Mine. When you pass through the waters, I will be with you; and through the rivers, they shall not overflow you. When you walk through the fire, you shall not be burned, nor shall the flame scorch you. For I am the LORD your God, the Holy One of Israel, your Savior; I gave Egypt for your ransom, Ethiopia and Seba in your place. Since you were precious in My sight, you have been honored, and I have loved you; therefore I will give men for you, and people for your life.
>
> —ISAIAH 43:1–4

With this revelation, my questions about where God was in the midst of my torment were quieted. I may never understand how evil works in this world, but my heart was becoming acquainted with the One who will judge for me. I knew Jesus would bring justice, not just because it is the right or legal thing to do, but because it is something a just God must do. He judges because the wrong committed against His children is personal to Him. When we harm one another, when the weak are crushed, when children are abused, Jesus takes it personally.

God's judgment is not just about punishing those who break His rules; it is a day He holds deeply in His heart (Isa. 63:4). I began to see that I could *not* ask Jesus to tone down His commitment to justice or quiet His wrath. I had to receive a truth in my mind and heart that Jesus is my Judge because He is my Bridegroom. I am His beloved bride, and He *will* fight for me. Again and again I saw the most terrifying passages about judgment in the Bible were ones in which God avenged harm done to His bride. Only when a bride is fought for and avenged can she lift her head in dignity and overcome what the oppressor sought to destroy in her heart. I was struck by the imagery in Revelation when God releases His most terrifying judgments on the harlot system that martyred His saints and sought to corrupt the heart of Jesus's bride.

> And I heard another voice from heaven saying, "Come out of her, my people, lest you share in her sins, and lest you receive of her plagues. For her sins have reached to heaven, and God has remembered her iniquities. Render to her just as she rendered to you, and repay her double according to her works; in the cup which she has mixed, mix double for her. In the measure that she glorified herself and lived luxuriously, in the same measure give her torment and sorrow; for she says in her heart, 'I sit as queen, and am no widow, and will not see sorrow.' Therefore her plagues will come in one day—death and mourning and famine. And she will be utterly burned with fire, for strong is the Lord God who judges her."
> —REVELATION 18:4–8

The Lord makes good on His promise and avenges His holy prophets and apostles in one day, bringing utter desolation to unrighteousness. (See Revelation 18:19–21.) In the subsequent chapter, Jesus is called the One who judges in righteousness and makes war. His eyes are "a flame of fire," and He is clothed with a robe dipped in blood (Rev. 19:11–13).

Freed by the Bridegroom Judge

Through my journey to overcome shame and see Jesus as one who will avenge the wrong done to me, I learned several important truths. I believe they will benefit anyone wanting to know the heart of Jesus as our Judge:

1. Vengeance is the Lord's business, not ours. We cannot know how God will bring forth His justice or take an account for the wrongs that were done. Hebrews 10:31 tells us that it is a fearful thing to fall into the hands of the living God. The truths of how God works His judgments are too terrifying and mysterious for us to even approach. Vengeance is not our domain (Rom. 12:18–20); our job is to give the case to the righteous Judge and know that He will make the wrong things right while giving every chance for mercy and repentance. (See 2 Thessalonians 1: 6-10.)

2. Someone will pay. Either Jesus Christ will accept the just punishment for the wrongs done to us, or the person who sinned against us will pay. The Bible says we all must appear

before God who will judge us (Rev. 20:13–15). No one is exempt. Thankfully, those who have accepted Christ are redeemed through His blood, and He has taken upon Himself the penalty for our wrongdoing. (See Ephesians 1:7; Colossians 1:14; 1 John 1:9.) God still judges the wrongs committed against us, but Jesus pays for them through His work on the cross instead of punishing the wrongdoers. Those who have not accepted Christ, however, will receive the weight of God's judgment.

3. God will not forget our case when we give it to Him. God is a just Judge, and He is angry with the wicked (Ps. 7:11). Throughout Scripture, He promises to remember their iniquity and punish their sins (Jer. 14:10; Hosea 8:13; 9:9; Ps. 90:7–9), and we know the Lord is faithful to keep His promises.

We can have complete assurance that the righteous Judge sees us and will fight for us, but that doesn't absolve us of the responsibility to forgive. Jesus displays an amazing power to forgive our sins, and He invites us to be like Him by forgiving others. For many who have suffered much, this seems almost impossible, but that was not the case with me. Read on, and I will explain how Jesus the Judge, the One whose eyes were lit with jealous fire, gave me a miraculous strength to forgive.

Chapter Ten

THE POWER TO FORGIVE

W HEN JESUS BEGAN to reveal Himself to me as Judge, I was apprehensive that I would begin to want God to unleash His wrath on those who had hurt me. I thought I might desire divine vengeance out of spite. The exact opposite happened as I continued to encounter the Jesus of the Bible. If you do the same, seeking not just some vague notion of Jesus the Judge but the real Jesus found through long and loving meditation in the Word, I know this revelation will bear the same fruit in your heart.

As Jesus revealed Himself to me as the righteous Judge, I caught a glimpse of the jealous fire in His eyes, which led me into a deeper realm of forgiveness than I had ever known. Understanding Jesus as the faithful witness (Rev. 1:5)—the One who saw and heard what no one else did—was what my heart had been yearning for all along. Upon seeing the fierce zeal in God's eyes for justice and His determination to make all the wrong things right, I found myself wanting to cry out for mercy for those who had harmed me.

In my study about forgiveness in light of the revelation of Jesus as the Judge I uncovered truths in the Bible that helped explain the work God was doing in my heart. I understood for the first time that the Lord would vindicate me, and that truth began to lead my heart toward real forgiveness. Jesus saw, heard, and would decide how to make things right. I matter so much to Him that His justice demands that someone must pay. Either Jesus will bear the guilt and consider the debt paid through His work on the cross if the person repents, or He will punish the wrongdoers when they stand before Him at the judgment. This is the reality that gripped my heart.

It is easy for well-meaning Christians to reduce forgiveness to sweeping transgressions under the rug, but this becomes catastrophic in the face of life's most evil atrocities. How can we sweep sexual abuse under the rug? How can we tell someone whose heart has been crushed, "Move on, and don't let the offense steal your joy"? Without the understanding that God will avenge the wrongs committed against us, the true meaning of forgiveness gets lost. For those who do not know Christ as the righteous Judge, a call to forgiveness can seem like a statement that Jesus doesn't care about what happened or that He is too magnanimous to be weighed down by our grievances. Instead of offering hope, forgiveness becomes a message of "get over it and move on."

Scripture offers an entirely different approach to forgiveness. Through forgiveness we release our case to a just Judge who will fight for us. We can forget what happened because we know God never will. Someone will pay for what was done. Any notions that Jesus is complacent in the face of sin and evil do not line up with Scripture's description of the terror awaiting the wicked when Christ returns. We see this clearly in the Book of Revelation.

Then the sky receded as a scroll when it is rolled up, and every mountain and island was moved out of its place. And the kings of the earth, the great men, the rich men, the commanders, the mighty men, every slave and every free man, hid themselves in the caves and in the rocks of the mountains, and said to the mountains and rocks, "Fall on us and hide us from the face of Him who sits on the throne and from the wrath of the Lamb!"

—REVELATION 6:14–16

When our understanding of true forgiveness is cheapened, we develop wrong ideas about Jesus that lessen our self-worth because we think we're not worth fighting for. All over the world, the poor, oppressed, and abused are longing for an answer to their pain and suffering. Jesus is that answer. He is the righteous Judge who will take an account, but too often the church is afraid of this truth.

Knowing Jesus as our Judge will not turn us into spiteful Christians who constantly speak negative words of judgment and condemnation. I can tell you from experience the exact opposite is true. When we understand that Jesus is the Judge, we realize an equally important truth—we are not! Jesus wants to heal our hearts with the revelation that He is the Judge, and He wants to give us truly good news for others who are oppressed.

Beloved, you will love Jesus so much more if you allow Him to be the Judge in your heart. I challenge you to acquaint yourself with the One who will render judgment on all of humanity, make an end of sin once and for all, and take an account of every wrong done.

Forgiving the Debt

Have you ever wondered why it is so difficult to forgive? It's human nature to want a guilty person to experience as much pain as they caused. This is why we so easily hold those who have wronged us in a choke hold until they make restitution, but this isn't God's heart for His children.

Jesus offered an amazing teaching on forgiveness one day when the apostle Peter asked Him how many times he should forgive his brother. "Up to seven times?" Peter asked (Matt. 18:21). Jesus responded by telling Peter a story that reveals the core of unforgiveness and helps explain why we must forgive others in order to receive forgiveness from the Father.

In the parable of the unforgiving servant, a king goes to settle accounts with his servants and finds one man who owes him ten thousand talents, which was a significant sum of money. The man was not able to pay, so the king commanded that the servant and his family be sold in order to repay the debt. The man begged the king to let him pay over time, and the Bible says the king was moved with compassion toward the man. Instead of letting him pay in installments, the king forgave the debt altogether.

Of course, the story doesn't end there. After his debt had been forgiven, the servant discovered that another man owed him a hundred denarii, a significantly smaller amount of money. The servant roughed the man up and demanded that the debt be repaid immediately. But, unable to pay, the man begged for mercy, just as the servant had sought mercy from the king.

But the servant refused to show pity and had the man thrown in jail. When the king learned what had happened, he was so angry he had the servant delivered to the torturers until he could repay his original debt. Jesus said this is how the Father would respond to anyone who does not forgive his brother from his heart (Matt. 18: 21–35). Mankind has a propensity to put those who have wronged us in a choke hold until we get just recompense. When we feel we have lost our worth or dignity, we often seek to reclaim it by force. If that's not possible, we want to at least keep our hands around our oppressor's throat so he will experience some penalty. This is because we don't believe anyone will recover what we have lost.

Yet understanding Jesus as our Judge gives us a totally different perspective. It enables us to leave room for God to right the wrongs and to trust that our heavenly Judge will make sure we have what we need. (See Romans 12:18–20.) When we look to Jesus as the One whose opinions matter most, we realize that nothing can separate us from the love of God or change our identity as His children. This means that nothing of real value can be stolen that God cannot return to us double.

Whether the offense is great or small, forgiveness really is not an option. In the parable of the unforgiving servant, Jesus reminds us that He forgave the greatest offense any human being can commit—participating in sin, which separates us from God. Jesus has forgiven not only our small infractions and minor debts but also every wrong we've ever done. And then He graciously gives us an eternal dividend—double for our trouble (Isa. 61:7). If we truly understand what Christ has given us, we will express that gratitude by forgiving others as He forgave us (Eph. 4:31–32).

The same principle is laid out in the Sermon on the Mount, when Jesus instructs His followers to show mercy, forgive, and be careful of the measure they use when judging others. (See Matthew 5–7.) Jesus explains that the law we put others under is the law we put ourselves under. (See Matthew 6:14–15.) The Bible says, "Judge not, that you be not judged. For with what judgment you judge, you will be judged; and with the measure you use, it will be measured back to you" (Matt. 7:1–2).

It is self-deception to tell yourself you are living beneath the mercy, patience, and forgiveness of Christ if you do not extend that same grace to others. Failing to extend mercy to others is evidence that we do not understand the level of grace God extended to us through His redemptive work on the cross. He reached into the depravity of our condition, took our sins upon Himself, and paid our debt, wiping clean the slate of offenses that kept us separated from the Father.

Because of what Jesus did, we can know Him as our Bridegroom and Judge and enter into His kingdom. It is those who reject Christ's work at Calvary and the Holy Spirit's continuing work of grace who will be subject to the weight of His judgment.

Christianity is the only religion that truly empowers people to acknowledge the wrong done and expect Jesus to bring vindication yet forgive the wrongdoer and pray that God's mercy would prevail. This simply is not possible outside of Jesus. Anyone can sweep things under the rug or tell a wounded person to "get over it," but that is not the answer Christ brings. He reaches into the deepest places of our hearts and does a deep work of healing that allows us to forgive and even pray that those who wronged us will not to have to experience God's fierce wrath.

When we settle in our hearts that justice will come, whether or not anyone saw what happened, we will be able to look with gratitude toward a righteous Judge and experience a supernatural pull toward forgiveness that seeks to make Jesus's mercy famous.

Making Jesus's Mercy Famous

At the beginning of my journey to know Jesus as the righteous Judge, I felt the Holy Spirit invite me to enter my first ever forty-day fast. I sensed the Lord wanted me to pray about reconciling with the minister who had abused me when I was a child. This seemed unthinkable to me at this point in my journey. I couldn't imagine God even wanting to work in someone who had unleashed so much destruction in my life and in the lives of so many others. But the Holy Spirit's invitation was too clear for me to dismiss, so I made this the focus of my prayers during the forty days.

At the beginning of the fast, I prayed for reconciliation dutifully; it was something I simply needed to get out of the way every day. I woke up in the morning, knelt briefly, and rushed through the sentence, "God, I pray for reconciliation between me and the person who wronged me. Amen." I then exhaled in relief thinking, "Great, I am done," and I went about my day.

As the days went by, I grew weaker and needed more and more focus to press through the fast. I was working full-time as a waitress in a Mexican restaurant and attending Bible school. Consuming only liquids with my busy schedule was wearing me out, and I had to remind myself why I was on this fast. I found myself talking to Jesus throughout the day while handing out tacos and nachos. "Jesus, I am more hungry for reconciliation with the person who wronged me than I am for this food I am serving."

With my defenses down because of the physical toll the fast was taking on me, God really began to do a deep work in my heart. A vision for reconciliation began to surface in my mind. I pictured what it would look like if the abuser and I were ever able to testify together of God's mercy—victim and victimizer speaking of the power of Jesus's blood to bring forgiveness and healing.

What began as dutiful thirty-second prayers turned into hours of weeping and groaning in intercession through several prayer times each day. Jesus was softening my heart and pulling out a root of unforgiveness, while also removing the trauma and terror I felt from the abuse I suffered at this person's hands. I felt as though Jesus had worked a creative miracle in my heart when, for the first time in my life, I didn't feel the deep bitterness I had carried for as long as I could remember.

At the end of the fast, I was filled with a desire to track

down the person who had abused me, tell him what Jesus had done in my heart, and extend God's mercy to him. This man was very close to my family, but I hadn't seen or spoken to him in a very long time. But after having received a breakthrough in my heart, I couldn't wait to see him and speak with him. I prayed for the Lord to open up an opportunity for me to meet with him, and God did.

One night when I was driving in a car with a friend of mine, I told her that I was about to have an opportunity to meet with the person who abused me the worst as a child. Looking out the car window into the starry night, I said to my friend, "Imagine how famous Jesus's mercy would be if He restored the person who abused me and the other children as well? I feel God's love for him so strongly. I just don't know how I can show him how I feel and how Jesus feels about him."

A thought came into my mind that seemed almost ridiculous. What if I washed his feet? Immediately I felt joy bubble up inside of me. It would be awesome to get to wash his feet from a heart free of bitterness. I didn't feel like I had to do it, not by any means, but I felt a strong desire to wash his feet. I thought, "Jesus, would You really have me do this?" I worried that maybe I was taking things too far. Perhaps this was an unhealthy thing for me to do.

Without telling my friend what I was thinking, I asked her to pray and see if God spoke anything to her about what I should do to show the abuser the love of Jesus. A few minutes of silence went by before she turned to me and said, "I don't know, but one line of a worship song keeps coming to my mind that talks about pouring out love and washing Jesus's feet." Tears of joy streamed down my face, God had seen my heart, and I knew that He had given me a way to show His love to someone who needed it more than anyone I knew.

Forgiving the Unthinkable

The day came. I remember sitting in the room waiting for the person to walk in. I had feared and hated this man all of my life, even when I was rejecting the memories of the abuse. At that time, I felt incredible shame for having such negative emotions toward a minister my family and so many others loved and respected.

I will never forget how I felt the moment he walked into the room. The only way I can describe it is to say that my heart leaped with love for him. I didn't feel an ounce of hatred, anger, bitterness, or fear. The thought that went through my mind was, "There is the man You love, God." I was able to see him through God's eyes, as a broken man who was in as much need of Jesus's mercy as I was.

As we sat down, I told him I forgave him for the specific wrongs he committed against me. Then I placed my hand on his shoulder and began to pray for God's blessing on him. I spoke with my whole heart, "Jesus's blood is enough for everything you have done to me and to others. I speak that over you as one of the ones you harmed. His blood is enough!"

I felt such a heavy burden lift from my heart, and my countenance lit up with joy, I remember asking him, "Can I wash your feet?" I had to ask him twice because it was so shocking for him to hear that from me. He nodded and looked baffled as I ran to the bathroom and came back with a basin of water and a towel. I felt so much joy and exhilaration. I remember thinking, "These are the most beautiful feet I have ever seen!"

Jesus's love had made my abuser's feet beautiful. I hope to have many glorious moments with Jesus in this life, but if I see the dead raised or millions come to salvation, I doubt it will feel any more precious to me than the moment I washed the feet of the person who hurt me the most. I looked up to heaven with an expression on my face that only my Father could fully read. Only He could know the magnitude of that moment when my heart was free to display the mercy of Jesus.

Have you ever had the opportunity to make Jesus's mercy famous? Have you ever experienced the sheer joy of truly loving your enemies? I am not just talking about refraining from retaliation. I am speaking of something much deeper and much more precious in the heart of God.

Jesus prayed that the very love the Father has for His own Son would be in us (John 17:26). With all of my heart, I encourage you to take Jesus up on His offer to fill your heart with love for the Bridegroom and to put that love on display in the darkest places. This is where God's love shines brightest. It is through knowing Jesus as Judge that we are finally able to release our oppressors from the choke holds we grasped in our attempt to seek vindication on our terms.

When our hearts are set free and we know our worth before God, we can begin the journey of displaying the mercy of our heavenly Father in the face of wrongs committed against us, both small and great. Then the glorious games begin as we receive the exhilarating opportunity to make Jesus's mercy famous and see the hardest hearts turn to Christ.

Finding the Strength to Forgive

The Lord has done a miraculous work of healing in my life, and He can do the same for anyone who will allow Him to reach those deep levels of pain. I know forgiving can be difficult; some people even seem to think it means denying the wrong committed against them or the effect it has had on them. This is completely untrue. Forgiveness is many things, but it is not an invitation to bury one's head in the sand. It is the response of someone who realizes how much the Bridegroom loves His bride and knows He will vindicate the wrongs done.

To summarize what we have been discussing in this chapter and to correct some of the misconceptions about forgiveness, I have listed several of attributes of forgiveness. I pray these truths will sink into your heart and lead you on a journey toward true transformation.

- Forgiveness is the response of a comforted heart.

- Forgiveness is the privilege of one who is vindicated and worth much.

- Forgiveness is the final freedom from victimization.

- Forgiveness is the external gesture of internal dignity.

- Forgiveness is the proof that we understand what we ourselves have received from God.

- Forgiveness is the overflow of a heart that has already found justice.

- Forgiveness is not a one-time event that we cross off of our list. It is a road that we must decide again and again to stay on.

Through forgiveness, we can find true freedom from bitterness and shame, but this is not the primary reason we forgive. As believers, our purpose for forgiving runs much deeper:

- We forgive because it displays God's power in our lives. It is nothing short of miraculous to no longer hate someone who wronged us and to even be able to intercede for him or her.

- We forgive because we need mercy ourselves, and God gives us the level of mercy we give to others. The Bible says in Matthew 6:14–15, "If you forgive men their trespasses, your heavenly Father will also forgive you. But if you do not forgive men their trespasses, neither will your Father forgive your trespasses."

- We forgive because it gives us the opportunity to make Jesus's mercy famous in the earth. We can know the joy of loving our enemies and manifesting Christ to a lost and hurting world through works we could only accomplish through the power of the Holy Spirit.

- We forgive because it allows us to imitate the One we love and get to know Him more. We love God because He first loved us (1 John 4:19), and it is this love He empowers us to share with others.

Arise, Zion!

Isaiah 51 paints a picture of a broken people. The children of Israel had been trampled in their affliction, literally walked on in the street. (See Isaiah 51:21–23.) But the Lord tells His children to arise, shake off the dust, and put on her strength because He is coming to redeem them. (See Isaiah 52:1–6.) We then see the bride of Christ fully restored in dignity and worth, lifting her voice with the good news she has received.

> Break forth into joy, sing together, you waste places of Jerusalem! For the Lord has comforted His people, He has redeemed Jerusalem. The Lord has made bare His holy arm in the eyes of all the nations; and all the ends of the earth shall see the salvation of our God.
>
> —Isaiah 52:9–10

Suffering and pain have left many of us feeling as though we are lying on the ground, stepped on and crushed. Yet part of our healing lies in this: we realize that we are not to fear man or oppression but God Himself, the mighty Judge who calls us to arise and shake off the dust. We must shake ourselves from the oppressor's victimization and belittling, shake ourselves from deriving our identity from what happened to us, shake ourselves from the respect and dread we give to the sins others committed against us and that we commit against ourselves.

Jesus is crying out, "I am bigger! And by My blood you are bigger too! Arise, shake yourself from the dust, and loose yourself from the bonds of your neck." I am convinced that more than raising the dead and healing the sick, what we need in this hour is the faith to believe we can rise above the enemies within our own souls.

The Lord has filled me with joy and has given me the privilege of making the good news of Jesus known as well as interceding for others to receive this freedom in their hearts. God is looking for those who will arise, shake themselves from the dust, and comfort others with the comfort they have received, the comfort that comes only from knowing Jesus the Judge.

Chapter Eleven

TURN BACK TO GOD

THE TRUTH OF Christ's coming judgment became an even greater reality to me one day while I was in prayer. On September 29, 2002, I was at home in my bedroom praying for a friend who needed guidance about some leadership transitions when I had an encounter with the Lord that changed my life.

As I was praying, suddenly I became aware of an increasing presence of the Lord. What the Bible calls "the spirit of the fear of the Lord" began to increase in my room. I began to feel a reverential awe of the Lord and couldn't help but tremble as I realized how small I was before the God who knows and sees all.

I continued to pray and thanked the Lord for the presence of the Holy Spirit. Soon I began to feel that there was some kind of message or encounter God wanted to give me, and I knew that whatever was about to happen was not just about me. Feeling inadequate to receive the magnitude of what I felt Jesus wanted to reveal, I asked my roommate who was in another room to come intercede for me.

As she prayed, she began to feel the heat and fire of the Holy Spirit and eventually left me alone with the Lord while she continued to seek God in the next room. I was fully awake and sitting on the edge of my bed when suddenly I was taken into an open vision. It was as if I was dreaming, but I was fully awake. Yet I was completely caught up in the events God was revealing to me and immersed in every detail.

In the vision, I found myself on a huge boat. It seemed to be an enormous cruise liner. I was on the deck, and everyone else was down below. I was so tiny compared to the size of the ship that it seemed thousands of people could have fit just on the deck. I was a tiny speck standing at the front of the boat looking out to the ocean as we sped along.

Straight ahead of us, stretching out as far as I could see, was the most terrifying storm you could imagine. A frightening mix of wind and lightning spanned the ocean as far as the eye could see. It was growing in fierceness and devastating power as it seemed to draw everything around it into its destructive vortex. The phrase "destruction from the Almighty" was ringing in my spirit. Later I looked up the phrase and found the following verses, which describe what God's judgment day is like.

> Wail, for the day of the LORD is at hand! It will come as destruction from the Almighty. Therefore all hands will be limp, every man's heart will melt, and they will be afraid. Pangs and sorrows will take hold of them; they will be in pain as a woman in childbirth; they will be amazed at one another; their faces will be like flames. Behold, the day of the LORD comes, cruel, with both wrath and fierce anger, to lay the land desolate; and He will destroy its sinners from it.
> —ISAIAH 13:6–9

It was clear to me that there was no way to maneuver around this storm as its width spanned endlessly to the left and right. Nor was there any way to remove the storm from our path. There also was no question that anyone or anything that entered this storm was headed for certain destruction. The only hope for this boat and its passengers was for it to somehow turn around and reverse its course. The water around the boat was already choppy, and as we inched closer the waves began to increase. The wind and waves were ferocious, much like the prophet Jeremiah's description of the Lord's fury.

> Behold, a whirlwind of the LORD has gone forth in fury—a violent whirlwind! It will fall violently on the head of the wicked. The anger of the LORD will not turn back until He has executed and performed the thoughts of His heart. In the latter days you will understand it perfectly.
>
> —JEREMIAH 23:19–20

Because no one on deck could see where the boat was headed, I decided to jump overboard and try to turn the ship around myself. It may sound like a ridiculous remedy, but it was the only thing I thought to do, and somehow I felt I had the power to accomplish this. I jumped into the stormy water and started swimming toward the front of the boat. I was a tiny person compared to this massive ship, yet I felt capable of changing the direction of this vessel. Swimming through the dangerous waters, I reached the front, grabbed the bow of the boat, and began to push the ship while shouting with a commanding voice, "Turn! Turn! Turn! You've got to turn!"

As I continued in prayer, a clear picture began to unfold to me. The boat was America, and it was heading into the judgments of a righteous God. God could not change who He is or be less than righteous in His requirements of our nation, but through intercession America could be turned. I did not feel hopeless, but I did feel desperate. I kept pushing the boat while screaming, "Turn!"

This vision recurred three times for the next hour. Each time the truths were the same, but my prayers took on a different focus. The first time my burden was for America, and I began to cry out for the nation to change its course and avoid this terrifying collision with a righteous God. The second time, my burden was for the church, which was being swept along by the current of a sinful culture and was also on a collision course with God. The third time, God was burdening me for my own community at the International House of Prayer in Kansas City.

A spirit of preaching and intercession came on me. I started shouting, "Turn," and then began to preach: "If you do not feel yourself rebelling and resisting the general flow of the direction you and others around you have taken, then you are not following the Lord. If you desire to be on the right side of the Judge, *turn*! If you are not causing others around you to alter their direction, you are not a prophetic witness, for this is the call. Our job as intercessors and prophetic people is this: to turn ourselves, then turn our cities and nation, the Western church, the countries of the world—cause them to turn."

I went from preaching to intercession there in my room as I remained in the grip of this vision. Prophecy never seemed clearer to me than in that moment. After hearing so many different definitions for prophetic ministry, I felt I was being hit right between the eyes with Jesus's real purpose for it: to call people to turn to Him. (See 2 Kings 17:13.) I was tiny compared to this massive boat, but a spirit of intercession was on me as I labored in prayer, crying out for this ship to turn. With my eyes closed, I had entered into the vision so deeply I couldn't pull out of it.

The Two Torches

Then just as suddenly as the vision had begun, I was released from its grip. Thrown back into the surroundings of my room, I opened my eyes, picked myself up off the floor, and sat on the edge of my bed. My first thought was, "What on earth was that?" But as soon as the question crossed my mind, the encounter went to a whole new level. With my eyes wide open, I looked across my room and saw Jesus standing in the corner of my bedroom. I know that in this life there is no way that we can see the full glory of the Lord Jesus and live. This was a small glimpse of Him, but it was enough to overwhelm me.

No matter how hard I tried, I couldn't get low enough; if I could have crawled under the carpet, I would have done so. Jesus was standing on the other side of my room, and there was lightning coming from His face, making it seem as if

His countenance was all light. It was terrifying. It seemed as though the lightning was actually shooting out from His face, and I felt it strike my body. I was knocked down onto the floor, and each ray of light that shot out at me seemed to leave me even more overwhelmed with the glory and greatness of Jesus.

I cried out at the top of my lungs. My roommate, who was in the other room, later said I sounded like I was dying, but she knew the Lord was doing something, so she didn't interrupt what was taking place. The experience reminded me of the scene in Matthew 28 when Jesus rose from the dead.

> And behold, there was a great earthquake; for an angel of the Lord descended from heaven, and came and rolled back the stone from the door, and sat on it. His countenance was like lightning, and his clothing as white as snow. And the guards shook for fear of him, and became like dead men.
>
> —MATTHEW 28:2–4

In the vision of Jesus, a sword of white light was coming out of His mouth, like the one described in Revelation 1:16, and He Himself was a flame of fire. Fire and light were everywhere, and their brightness seemed to hurt my eyes. I was lying on the floor with my face down on the carpet trying not to look up at this glorious vision of Jesus. I was terrified that I would not live through this divine encounter. I had rug burns and bruises on my arms and legs for quite a while after the vision because of how forcefully I dove onto the floor to get as low as I could.

I was incapable of looking up at the face of the One who stood before me, and I had determined not to move but to keep my face on the ground and let Him do whatever He wanted with me. The apostle John, the one to whom Jesus told His secrets, had an encounter that far surpassed the glimpse of Jesus I experienced that night in September. John records in Revelation that:

> His feet were like fine brass, as if refined in a furnace, and His voice as the sound of many waters; He had in His right hand seven stars, out of His mouth went a sharp two-edged sword, and His countenance was like the sun shining in its strength. And when I saw Him, I fell at His feet as dead. But He laid His right hand on me, saying to me, "Do not be afraid; I am the First and the Last."
>
> —REVELATION 1:15–17

The encounter that took place in my room that night was not a dream; it was real. I felt the fierceness of the Lord in a way I had never experienced before and haven't since. When Jesus spoke, it sounded like a roar coming from the direction where He was standing, but it also seemed to come from deep within my own spirit. The words shook me to the core. He said, "Stand and deliver." I thought to myself, "Oh, God. Don't let this be a literal command! There is no way I can stand to my feet right now."

In my spirit, I knew Jesus was telling me that this was a word I must hear and deliver. I knew this life-changing encounter was not just for me. He was giving me a message for the church, and I did not have the option to retreat from this encounter. I didn't stand up—I was incapable of doing so—but I was able to move to a kneeling position before the Lord and look up to Jesus. Encounters that seem difficult to even endure are described in the Scriptures. One such example is the prophet Daniel's terrifying experience with an angel in Daniel 10.

> I lifted my eyes and looked, and behold, a certain man clothed in linen, whose waist was girded with gold of Uphaz! His body was like beryl, his face like the appearance of lightning, his eyes like torches of fire, his arms and feet like burnished bronze in color, and the sound of his words like the voice of a multitude. And I, Daniel, alone saw the vision, for the men who were with me did not see the vision; but a great terror fell upon them, so that they fled to hide themselves. Therefore I was left alone when I saw this great vision, and no strength remained in me; for my vigor was turned to frailty in me, and I retained no strength. Yet I heard the sound of his words; and while I heard the sound of his words I was in a deep sleep on my face, with my face to the ground. Suddenly, a hand touched me, which made me tremble on my knees and on the palms of my hands. And he said to me, "O Daniel, man greatly beloved, understand the words that I speak to you, and stand upright, for I have now been sent to you." While he was speaking this word to me, I stood trembling.
> —DANIEL 10:5–11

As my terrifying encounter with Jesus continued, I was able to look back up at Him, and I saw Him standing before me as clear as I have seen any other human being in my life. He was holding two burning torches, one in each hand. Looking at them, the Holy Spirit spoke to my heart so that I knew without any doubt what these torches were. One torch was the fear of the Lord—the reverential awe of the Lord that leads us to holiness. The other was "the first commandment," which is the power to love God with all that we are. As He stood there with these two torches burning red hot, He shouted, "Give this to My people."

He spoke it as if to say that we as the church have been asking Jesus for many things—church growth strategies, ways to increase our finances and find happiness in life, principles for walking in God's anointing for miracles, and much more. It was as if Jesus was saying that in all of our asking there are two things He would like us to seek before everything else. Jesus wanted to give His church the power to fear Him alone and to love Him with all their heart, mind, and strength. (See Matthew 22:37.)

When He said, "Give this to My people," He stepped across the entire span of my bedroom in one step and thrust the two torches into my very being. As soon as He did this, I felt fire from the inside out, and I experienced my first level of revelation about the fear of the Lord and the first commandment. Then the Lord said, "They seem a little foreign, don't they?" I began to sob all the more, grieving, and He said, "Yes, like two foreigners in the land, so are the fear of the Lord and the first commandment."

As I wept, I was gripped with an awareness of how foreign the first commandment and the fear of the Lord are in this day and age, this nation, my life, and even our ministry in Kansas City. I felt like I was meeting two strangers for the first time. It was as though the fear of the Lord and the first commandment were part of a whole other reality that we were completely unaware of.

I began to cry out in grief, trying to understand how these values could be as foreign to me and other believers as I now understood them to be. Prayer had been a major focus of my life for several years, and I was a leader in a community that seeks to walk out radical Christianity together. Yet the fear of the Lord and a real demonstration of the first commandment were completely new to me.

One Love, One Fear

Revelation and living understanding had come to me in one moment. All over the world, people gather for prayer and pursue the Lord radically as the Holy Spirit moves in many regions. Yet we are all still far from the pure fear of the Lord and the first commandment fully gripping us and being released in our hearts and our communities. We do not know this kind of fierce love and awesome fear.

What are the love of God and the fear of the Lord? These became very real to me as I began to understand what Jesus was looking for in my own heart and in His church. The first commandment speaks of a radical love for God that requires spiritual violence as God's love takes primacy in our hearts. The fear of the Lord refers to a lovesick trembling that purifies the heart of Jesus's bride, leads us to a deeper knowledge of who God is, and shakes us from our complacency and compromise. The Lord was telling me that despite all of our religious activities, we have lost sight of the things Jesus wants the most.

When the Lord thrust these two torches into my being and said, "Give these to My people," I did not suddenly begin manifesting holy fear and fierce love at the level God desires. There is no cheating God; I will be pursuing these two keys to God's heart for the rest of my life. Receiving the torches was my first step toward being consumed with what Jesus is actually looking for in His bride.

I continue to be struck by the simplicity of what the Lord requires from us. We make it so complicated, and He has made it so clear. Love the Lord your God and fear Him only. One love and one fear—He made it absolutely clear. Deuteronomy 30 says it plainly:

> For this commandment which I command you today is not too mysterious for you, nor is it far off. It is not in heaven, that you should say, "Who will ascend into heaven for us and bring it to us, that we may hear it and do it?" Nor is it beyond the sea, that you should say, "Who will go over the sea for us and bring it to us, that we may hear it and do it?" But the word is very near you, in your mouth and in your heart, that you may do it. See, I have set before you today life and good, death and evil, in that I command you today to love the LORD your God, to walk in His ways, and to keep His commandments, His statutes, and His judgments, that you may live and multiply; and the LORD your God will bless you in the land which you go to possess.
>
> —DEUTERONOMY 30:11–16

When the Lord began to speak to me again, He said, "Without these two, you will be just like the rest." It began to ring in my spirit that He was speaking about every area of our lives and public ministry. In everything we do and in all that we are, both personally and corporately, Jesus is looking for the fear of the Lord and the love of God. Many times we live our lives or lead our ministries like people who have studied for the wrong test, not knowing what Jesus really wants of us. We assume that He expects us to succeed in a thousand ways, be productive, and receive recognition from others, when actually He longs for something much simpler: that we would love Him with all our hearts and tremble before the God to whom we will all give an account.

Without the fear of the Lord, without the first commandment burning in every area of our lives and ministries, we become just like the rest. This speaks of the reality that many Christians know Jesus personally, we may even accomplish some of His will corporately, but ultimately we may not be that helpful to the Lord. Jesus describes this circumstance in His Sermon on the Mount when He reveals two categories of believers. They all are in His kingdom but are in differing degrees of greatness, and therefore are less or more helpful in accomplishing Jesus's purposes.

> Whoever therefore breaks one of the least of these commandments, and teaches men so, shall be called least in the kingdom of heaven; but whoever does and teaches them, he shall be called great in the kingdom of heaven.
>
> —MATTHEW 5:19

The first commandment will be first place in the heart of Jesus's bride before He returns (see Revelation 22:7), but the transition through which the church will begin to seek first His kingdom will be radical and costly. It will require spiritual violence for us to realign our priorities and step into simple devotion to Christ. The Bible talks about this spiritual violence in Matthew 11:12: "From the days of John the Baptist until now the kingdom of heaven suffers violence, and the violent take it by force."

In saying, "You will be just like the rest," Jesus was settling the issue about what He is looking for in His church. Churches that do not embrace the fear of the Lord and the first commandment as their top priorities may still be able to hang on to their members, but they will not be helpful in preparing the earth for the events that will occur before Christ's return.

In Matthew 26:36 Jesus told the majority of His disciples, "Sit here while I go and pray over there." Then He took Peter, James, and John aside and shared with them the deeper matters on His heart and invited them to partner with Him in prayer. (See Matthew 26:38.) In the same way, Jesus is inviting His church to watch and pray with Him, and even to partner with Him as He brings forth judgments that prepare the earth for His coming. Even among the church, some will be positioned for maximum intimacy and partnership with Jesus, and others will not. In essence Jesus was saying, "Don't settle for the status quo, or you will be like the many who are saved but are not entering into deep friendship with Me in this hour of human history."

Jesus continued to speak in the vision, and though the revelation was new, I later recognized that His words came directly from Scripture. He said to me, "Without these two, you will be just like the rest. I will turn my face against you, break down your walls, and shatter the fruit of your labors." (See Ezekiel 14:6–9; 13:9–16; Deuteronomy 28:14–15, 33.) When Jesus spoke these words I was shocked to realize that He is just as much in the business of shutting down churches and ministries as He is in raising them up.

This word was devastating. At the time I received this vision, one of our fledgling prayer ministry's most beloved scriptures was Isaiah 62:6: "I have set watchmen on your walls." We felt our whole calling was to set watchmen, or intercessors, on the walls who would cry out for God's purposes to be accomplished in Israel and the ends of the earth.

Yet through this divine encounter, I understood Jesus to be saying to us at the International House of Prayer, "Great. You have organized your worship teams and your prayer shifts, but without the fear of the Lord and the first commandment values, it means nothing to Me. It is just one more thing that I have to tear down in order to do My work in My bride and in the nations of the world."

The next phrase the Lord spoke hit home as well. Jesus said He would "shatter the fruits of our labors" if we did not prioritize loving Him and fearing Him both as an organization and as individuals. I found the same truths in Ezekiel 13:10-12:

Because they have seduced My people, saying, "Peace!" when there is no peace—and one builds a wall, and they plaster it with untempered mortar—say to those who plaster it with untempered mortar, that it will fall. There will be flooding rain, and you, O great hailstones, shall fall; and a stormy wind shall tear it down. Surely, when the wall has fallen, will it not be said to you, "Where is the mortar with which you plastered it?"

As we build our ministries and churches, are we just creating more man-focused structures that Jesus has to fight with in order to achieve His purposes for His bride? The good often becomes the enemy of the best, and Jesus will actually war against much of the scaffolding we feel is necessary for our churches and ministries because it is distracting our hearts from loving God.

True Intercession

Many of you may be shocked at the fierceness of Jesus's language in this encounter. I was too, but after I shared the vision with leaders in our ministry, we found that everything Jesus spoke truly does bear out in Scripture. Hearing this prophetic message released grace and strength to our community at the International House of Prayer in Kansas City and helped us focus on what matters most. After having this encounter with the Lord, I found that He was quoting Ezekiel 13 in several ways, as well as Jeremiah 23.

Both of these passages speak to those who are called to prophetically discern the signs of the times, rightly interpret God's activity in the moment of judgment, and call His people to turn from sin back to God. Those who are called to be intercessors and prophetic witnesses are required to have the word of the Lord in order to rightly understand the times in which we live and do everything in our power to see our generation turn to God. This is precisely what God is addressing in Ezekiel 13 and Jeremiah 23, which I believe Jesus was quoting throughout this entire encounter.

> Therefore thus says the Lord GOD: "I will cause a stormy wind to break forth in My fury; and there shall be a flooding rain in my anger, and great hailstones and fury to consume it. So I will break down the wall you have plastered with untempered mortar, and bring it down to the ground, so that its foundation will be uncovered; it will fall, and you shall be consumed in the midst of it. Then you shall know that I am the LORD. Thus will I accomplish My wrath on the wall and on those who have plastered it with untempered mortar; and I will say to you, 'The wall is no more, nor those who plastered it, that is, the prophets of Israel who prophecy concerning Jerusalem, and who see visions of peace for her when there is no peace,'" says the Lord GOD.
>
> —EZEKIEL 13:13–16

> For who has stood in the counsel of the LORD, and has perceived and heard His word? Who has marked His word and heard it? Behold, a whirlwind of the LORD has gone forth in fury—a violent whirlwind! It will fall violently on the head of the wicked. The anger of the LORD will not turn back until He has executed and performed the thoughts of His heart. In the latter days you will understand it perfectly. "I have not sent these

prophets, yet they ran. I have not spoken to them, yet they prophesied."

These shocking passages parallel each other and are addressing prophetic ministers, intercessors, and messengers who are called to understand and interpret God's activity in an hour of judgment. How could God break down our own ministry walls as Ezekiel 13:9–16 describes? When the spiritual walls of our ministries and churches are built with mortar that is false, mortar that says "peace, peace" when there is no peace, Jesus will shake all of our efforts until they line up with His truth.

All over the world God is raising up prayer ministries that are building walls of intercession to guard God's people on the day of the Lord. But Ezekiel 13:5 speaks to those very ministries, warning them to be careful and attentive, because "you have not gone up into the gaps to build a wall for the house of Israel to stand in the battle on the day of the LORD."

As faithful witnesses, we must cry out with a clear voice against issues of sin and say, "No! The Lord will not bless and keep a nation that has departed from Him in every imaginable way. America—including the church—must turn back to God!"

Jesus cannot be less than who He is; He is a righteous God. It is not enough for Christians to wave an American flag and claim that our forefathers made covenants before the Lord or that we have a godly heritage in this nation and rely on those things to make up for our sins. None of that will save

America. None of that will bring peace to this nation. There is one reality that will bring blessing to the United States, and that is repentance before a holy God. In order for that to take place, a prophetic people must arise who intercede according to true knowledge of the Lord and expose the many gaps in our nation's wall of safety that have left us in a predicament only repentance can fix.

The fierceness of God's rebuke in Ezekiel 13 and Jeremiah 23 corresponds with the responsibility He has given those in the body of Christ who are truly called to be forerunners and prophetic intercessors to help prepare the way for Christ's return. The Lord will have many of these intercessors around the world who are just a step ahead in their understanding of the unique dynamics of the End Times. Therefore they will be equipped to coach the body of Christ to respond in the fear of the Lord before Jesus the Judge and in the first commandment before Jesus the Bridegroom.

These two faces of Jesus, which the Holy Spirit will emphasize before the Lord returns, must provoke the right response in us as we mourn in repentance before the Judge and rejoice in love before the Bridegroom. The generation that lived during the first coming of Jesus was unresponsive and failed this test (see Matthew 11:16–17), but the Word of God gives us hope that His church will be shining with the fear of the Lord and the first commandment before His second coming. (See Jeremiah 23:20; Daniel 12:3.)

The words that Jesus spoke to me were sharp and clear, cutting through all the fog right to my very core. He finished His message about the fear of the Lord and the love of God with one more phrase that was meant to provoke an even deeper outrage in my own soul. He said, "Go ahead and be like the rest if you desire." Again, it may sound like Jesus was too intense here for this message to be consistent with His Word, but whatever the mystery of His tactic is, I can tell you that this phrase, like nothing He had said up to that point, caused me to rise up in intercession.

I began to cry out on behalf of our prayer ministry, and I began to say, "Lord, that is not our desire. We desire You. O God, we desire to be changed by You, Lord Jesus. You are our desire. It is not our desire to be like the rest." I was weeping and crying out, "Look upon our house with mercy. Look upon our house with mercy, O God."

Chapter Twelve

THE HOUR OF GOD'S JUDGMENT

M Y ENCOUNTER WITH Jesus gripped my heart with a holy fear. I felt the weight of the word the Lord was speaking to me and knew my life would be forever changed by it, though I did not yet know to what extent. I was still kneeling on the floor of my bedroom interceding for our prayer ministry and the body of Christ when the Lord began to speak again, saying, "When will you realize with one heart and one mind that you are living in the land of My judgment? I have set My face against this nation, and I will not relent. I changed the atmosphere on September 11. Does anyone feel it? Does anyone perceive it? Behold, I set before you this day; I have made known My desire. Will you keep My Word? Will I find you burning with the fire of faith, with the fire of love and trembling?"

Then I was taken right back into the vision of the ship that needed to turn around. The Holy Spirit spoke to me, "The true voices will labor to turn the people, to change the direction. This is how I measure success in this hour." Jeremiah 23:22 came to my mind, "If they had stood in My counsel, and caused My people to hear My words, then they would have turned them from their evil way and from the evil of their doings."

I realized that the prophetic ministries in our nation have not known how to rightly interpret the events of September 11, 2001, and have strayed from the real purpose of the prophetic witness, which is to lead people closer to Jesus and further from sin. September 11 was meant to shake our nation and cause us to realize that our real problem does not lie with Osama bin Laden; it lies with God's righteous storm of judgment, which will keep hitting America precisely because Jesus loves us and is beckoning His people to awake and arise.

We need a good, old-fashioned revival in which the fear of the Lord is introduced to a generation that does not have a clue what it is. God is holding His prophetic intercessors and forerunners accountable to truly hear with clarity what He is doing in this hour and call the nations to turn. If He finds the fear of the Lord and the love of God in our hearts and in the center of our ministries, then we will have purchased the right to partner with Him in this hour. If we do not make the love of God and the fear of God central, we may be saved from eternal damnation, but we will not have the right to partner with Him in turning this nation and everyone He has given us to personally turn through our witness. This is a battle for our inheritance. It is a battle for friendship with Jesus.

The Lord is saying to us as a people: "I want You with Me. I am the Bridegroom Judge, and My heart is weeping right now over what I've released in your nation. Yet you are afraid even to speak of it. You are afraid even to acknowledge the reality that I have set My face against this nation, to acknowledge the reality that on September 11 the atmosphere changed in this nation, to acknowledge the reality that you have been found wanting as a nation. This is the hour of My judgments, and all of humanity is heading toward a storm right now."

Beloved, it is by His grace that He would give us a reality check about what is taking place in our nation right now. This is an hour that demands a response. I have been guilty in my own life of thinking that I would succeed as a forerunner if I simply knew that God's judgments are coming in a general way. But that is not enough!

What God is looking for is a response to the Bridegroom, a response to the Judge. He is longing for a people who will tremble at His Word. God has not called us to stand back with a smirk on our faces because we have knowledge of His plans and activities. He has called us to turn. He has called us to move from the current that is carrying the body of Christ into the judgments of the Lord. He has called us to repent, to go against the flow first in our personal lives by loving Him and trembling before the Judge and Bridegroom. Then we are to partner with Him in turning the body of Christ in this nation.

I want to stand before Him on that fearsome judgment day as one who helped turn many. I am not satisfied with anything less. I have been forever changed by the knowledge of the fear of the Lord and the first commandment.

A Word That Demands a Response

During my encounter with the Lord, the word of the Lord was clear. He has turned His face against this nation in judgment until we repent. He changed the atmosphere on September 11, and we, His people, must perceive it. We cannot shrink back from responding to this word and calling people to turn. We are accountable to respond to the word He has spoken.

There is no comfort or safety for those who will not stand against the opinions of the day and hear the true word of the Lord. God's face will come against us if we do not do so. Will we be saved? Will we be the beloved of the Lord? Will we be the bride of Christ? Will the Bridegroom be ravished over us? Absolutely, but we will stand before Him on that day having fallen short of the grace of God because we did not turn and because we turned no one. (See 1 Corinthians 3:9–15.)

What are you turning in your life? Who around you is turning back to God? That is all that matters. That is the word of the Lord right now: "Turn! Turn! Turn! Turn!" That is the only prophecy that can be given when the storm of the Lord is upon our beloved America. Yet some Christians accuse anyone who even hints at the fact that God may be releasing judgments or shakings upon our nation of having a negative or critical spirit. They claim that if we say that the Lord is releasing judgment, then somehow we are jinxing America or operating in unbelief. It is as if we think that if we don't acknowledge that God is judging us, we can somehow avoid it and be safe.

The body of Christ in America is putting her head in the sand like the proverbial ostrich. The fact that we are intercessors crying out for revival doesn't mean we shouldn't speak things that are negative. Beloved, I must plead with you. What we really should be concerned about is disagreeing with the word of the Lord and His assessment of our nation. The most negative thing we can do is to not stand in the counsel of the Lord, to be found lacking the fear of the Lord, and to be unresponsive to the Bridegroom's call.

Jesus speaks of this in Matthew 11 when He addresses the cities whose inhabitants were cold to the message of the Bridegroom, represented in this passage by the wedding flute and of the Judge, reflected in their mourning.

> But to what shall I liken this generation? It is like children sitting in the marketplaces and calling to their companions, and saying: "We played the flute for you, and you did not dance; we mourned to you, and you did not lament."
>
> —MATTHEW 11:16–17

Could God be speaking this to America and to the nations of the earth at this time? When the word of the Lord comes to us, Jesus demands a response. Even those of us who have studied the End Times are not immune to the dilemma Jesus was addressing in this passage in Matthew. We can actually be lulled into a state of false comfort because we have heard the message of what God plans to do. But hearing the message and even agreeing with it is not enough. We must respond.

The choice is ours. Will we be found turning people back to the Lord, or will we barely hang on to our salvation and turn no one? How tragic if we come to Him empty-handed on that day because we were unwilling to live a life that really compelled anyone to turn back to God. I cannot settle for being able to simply say that I understood a little bit about

God's judgments and His End Time plan. I don't want it to be said that I had no impact because I was not willing to bear the stigma of declaring what I knew to be true.

I want to live with a sense of urgency and a commitment to extravagant fasting and prayer. I do not want to say on that day that I was unable to hear the words of Jesus to my generation. I can't settle for having my heart closed to the burden of the Lord because of nationalistic pride or a failure to really seek the God of the Bible.

Come to Christ

Humbled and convicted by the word God was speaking to me, I knelt weeping in my bedroom, yet I had a new resolve to stand in God's counsel and be a faithful witness for Christ. I determined then to call many within my generation to turn back to God. Still, I felt overwhelmed by my own weaknesses and inadequacies. Yet in that moment, I felt Jesus begin to weep with me and to envelop me in His love. When I looked up, I saw the face that had been so fierce and terrifying was now filled with tenderness and love, and His arms were stretched out toward me.

He said, "Come. Come to Me, O weak ones. Come. I will gather you up. I will teach you. You deny My power to transform you by your undue, unrelenting focus on your weakness. Just come. Oh, come, weak ones, little ones. I can make you just like Me. You can be changed. Your wounds are not incurable. I am the Lord. I am the Lord. I am the Lord." Then I heard what sounded like a cry coming from a distance. It was a voice shouting, "Who will stand and be numbered with the righteous?"

The Lord was showing me that He wants us to cast aside all of our insecurities, weaknesses, and self-focus so we can rise up and call this nation to turn. I am convinced that too much introspection has caused madness in this generation. When we become so afraid of our own weaknesses, we don't allow ourselves to experience the joy of being transformed by the power of God. Too many Christians are not rising up as intercessors and prophetic messengers because they think they are not qualified enough or that it is presumptuous for us to accept God's call on our lives. They draw back, thinking, "That is for the anointed man or woman on the platform, not for me."

Jesus is saying, "Come to Me! I will take you! I want an entire people who stand in the counsel of the Lord. Your wounds are not incurable." I know my own weakness very well, but my weakness will not get the last word. His transforming power is stronger than my weakness.

That day in my room I felt the Lord's heart for the small band of weak and broken people who have gathered in Kansas City to pray at the International House of Prayer. Even now, though we have grown, we are still so weak. The Lord sees us as a weak, disoriented people gathered from all around the world, stumbling and fumbling and grappling with our little issues as He beckons us to enter a deeper place in His heart.

He is calling you to come to Him, to believe that your wounds are not incurable, that your weaknesses are no match for His power. Maybe we wouldn't say it outright, but many of us believe our weaknesses are too difficult for the Holy Spirit to transform, that somehow His power works for everyone except us. That is a lie from the pit of hell! The issues in our lives can seem so big, but Jesus is saying, "I have called you to something bigger than those issues in your life."

He beckons us to find His grace in our weaknesses and calls us to rise above all the little storms, such as who is or isn't giving us what we want, or how close or far we are from accomplishing our goals. Despite our fumbling and bumbling, Jesus is beckoning us into friendship, a greater grace, and a radical response to His Word that would cause many to turn to Him.

Somehow Jesus found you, as He did me. It wasn't because of our nobility. It was because of His grace. His grace is present so we can hear His voice asking us to simply come to Him, to turn to Him with all of our hearts. He speaks so that weak people like you and me can receive a new commissioning as we hear His words. Repent to Him, receive His mercy, and start fresh right now. You have a new building permit to construct your future with power. There is a new trumpet sound, a new resolve to turn others as we turn ourselves. We must turn others by the grace of God, not because it's our burden but because it's our opportunity.

We must fearlessly proclaim the hour we are in. We must demonstrate how reasonable it is to give oneself to fasting and prayer. We must share the beauty of abandoning oneself in the simplicity of loving God and fearing Him, removing all else to become arrows in God's hands that pierce the darkness in this generation. United in Him, we become as one arrow, hitting the target with great force. This is what Jesus is calling His body to in this hour.

Jesus is longing for us to come to the One who is meek and lowly of heart, the One who can give us rest for our souls (Matt. 11:28–29). Right now, no matter where you are, He will give you a new beginning, a new mercy. He is not intimidated by your brokenness; He stands with His arms wide open, calling you to simply come. Come like a child, come with your wounds, come with your questions—just come. He has the power to transform you in your weakness, and He will use the most broken among us to turn many back to His heart and prepare a generation for His return.

At a Crossroads

Beloved, this word from the Lord demands an answer. I believe Joel 2, which speaks of a moment of judgment, gives us a recipe for responding to this word.

> "Now, therefore," says the LORD, "turn to Me with all your heart, with fasting, with weeping, and with mourning." So rend your heart, and not your garments; return to the LORD your God, for He is gracious and merciful, slow to anger, and of great kindness; and He relents from doing harm. Who knows if He will turn and relent, and leave a blessing behind Him—a grain offering and a drink offering for the LORD your God? Blow the trumpet in Zion, consecrate a fast, call a sacred assembly; gather the people, sanctify the congregation, assemble the elders, gather the children and nursing babes.
>
> —JOEL 2:12–16

Great strength is being released to the people of God in this hour to be of one mind and heart concerning the judgments of the Lord. We find ourselves in the midst of a wicked and perverse generation, but the Lord has placed around us righteous ones who have stood, who have come out of the wickedness and have committed to fast and pray. I don't want to miss the destiny God has for me personally or for the ministry He has called me to. I encourage you to test and weigh the word given to me in the vision and to search the Scriptures concerning the meaning of this encounter.

These are the main points I would encourage you to pray over and respond to as the Lord leads:

1. *Cultivate the fear of the Lord.* Study the fear of the Lord in Scripture and meditate on the concept of Jesus as Judge. Then let the fear of the Lord release a new grace for holiness in your life and in the lives of those you influence.

2. *Put God's first commandment in first place.* Seek to love the Lord with all you are and all you have (Matt. 22:37; Mark 12:29–30), and meditate upon Jesus as your Bridegroom.

3. *Stand in God's counsel.* Make it a habit to ask the Lord what He is doing in this hour, and fill your heart and mind with the Word of God. Scripture has much to say about the events that will take place before Jesus returns and

how we can know His heart and turn many to righteousness.

4. *Stand in righteous community.* The encounter I had in 2002 ended with the Lord asking, "Who will stand and be numbered with the righteous?" To exemplify a radical lifestyle of responding to Jesus, we need one another. We can go much further in our quest to recover radical Christianity when we identify people with whom we can link arms in the midst of a crooked and perverse generation.

5. *Pray for your nation.* God spoke very clearly in the vision about America specifically because He was speaking to a group of intercessors in the United States. Yet every nation needs intercessors who will arise and seek to turn the boat around. We must remain hopeful that prayer can change the destiny of a nation and its people.

Chapter Thirteen

A CALL TO FRIENDSHIP WITH GOD

I N MATTHEW 26, we find one of the most powerful descriptions of friendship with God in the entire Bible. In this passage, Jesus was in the Garden of Gethsemane and called His disciples Peter, James, and John away with Him. Here is the progression: Jesus takes all the disciples with Him to the garden. Then He takes three aside and says to the others, "Sit here while I go and pray over there" (Matt. 26:36).

With these three disciples, Jesus shared His heart on a deeper level than He did with the general masses or even the other disciples, telling them that His soul was "exceedingly sorrowful, even to death" (Matt. 26:38). He asked them to watch and pray with Him while He cried out to the Father, asking that the cup of God's judgment pass from Him if that were possible.

The three men Jesus drew away with Him were not the mightiest or the most talented. In many respects, they were flawed, but that didn't stop Jesus from seeking them out to be part of His inner circle. Why? I am convinced that two things set Peter, James, and John apart from the others in Gethsemane that night.

First, they were insatiably hungry for more revelation from Jesus. John was a relentless lover of God. At the Last Supper, he only wanted to be close to the Lord to listen to every word that would come out of His mouth, and he is remembered in Scripture as the one whom Jesus allowed to lean on His chest. James too was in hot pursuit of his Lord and was one of the first to answer Jesus's call to follow Him. Similarly, Peter was the first disciple to recognize Jesus as the Christ; as a result the Lord called him a rock and used Peter mightily to build His church. (See Matthew 16:13–20.)

Second, these three disciples didn't draw back from the Lord in order to clean themselves up so they would appear godly and mature. Instead they were real with Jesus about their ambitions and problems and allowed Him to coach and rebuke them even if it meant looking foolish before others or having the other disciples mad at them.

In Luke 9, Jesus had to rebuke James and John for wanting to call down fire from heaven to consume a Samaritan village that rejected Him (Luke 9:53–54). He lovingly informed them that He came to save lives, not to destroy them. Perhaps more embarrassing was when James and John sent their mother to ask Jesus if her sons could sit to His left reigning over everyone forever. After this incident Jesus took James and John aside to explain that His economy isn't like the world's; those who desire to be great must become servants. (See Matthew 20:20–28.)

As for Peter, he had the courage to step out of a boat and walk on water when Jesus called him. But before he could reach his destination, he took his eyes off the Lord, began to focus on the wind and waves, and started to sink. When

Jesus rescued him, He chided the man He had called a rock for having so little faith (Matt. 14:28–31).

These disciples were all flawed. No one would deny that they had their faults. Yet they said yes to Jesus in the midst of their weakness and as a result were brought closer to Jesus than anyone else in Gethsemane that night.

When I read Matthew 26, I'm completely undone with longing to be a friend of God, to be someone with whom the Lord would share His deepest thoughts and emotions. I have wept and prayed so many hours over Jesus's directive, "Sit here while I go over there and pray." I don't want the Lord to ever say that to me. I don't want my heart to be too cold or my mind too cluttered that He can't share His heart with me.

The Heart of Prophecy

Our God cannot stand doing anything on the earth without allowing people to understand and perceive His heart. (See Amos 3:7.) He longs to make Himself known and desires friends who can help others understand and perceive His heart. One of my life's greatest desires is that by the grace of God I would be a faithful friend to Jesus and that I would win to Him many friends. One of my goals through this book is to encourage many of you in your friendship with Jesus. I remember how crushed I felt on September 11, 2001, when I realized how far I was from being a close friend of God's. I was just as shocked as everyone else by the vicious terrorist attack on the United States. My first reaction was, of course, horror at the lives lost. Then I wondered, "How does Jesus feel about this? Who was there to weep with Him?"

Although I am a full-time intercessor at the International House of Prayer in Kansas City and I feel called to pray for America and God's purpose in the earth as my primary occupation, I did not hear from the Lord about what would happen September 11. I didn't want to know the details for the sake of having information or proving to others that I heard from God, but my heart was grieved when the events of September 11 happened, and I wondered, "Did God have friends weeping and praying over this?" After the attacks, I remember sobbing and telling the Lord, "Jesus, I thought I was Your friend, but if I truly were Your friend, You would have told me!" In the silence, I felt the Holy Spirit's presence strongly, and I clearly felt the Lord say, "If you were My friend, I would have." This statement pierced my heart with devastating conviction, but it was not said with condemnation. I felt the Lord's love and kindness. The Holy Spirit started to minister to my heart, and I began to see things more clearly. I began to see how full my life was—all the noise and hustle and bustle. I had lost my quiet walk with Jesus. I had lost my listening heart. I had lost my desire to weep with Him and instead had gotten caught up with giving prophetic words and being excited about the nuances I was able to unpack out of the Word of God. In the midst of all this, I lost my place of friendship with Him. I didn't make time to weep with Him, so He wept alone.

I am very aware that several people did hear God's heart concerning September 11 and were found weeping with Him, both well-known ministers such as David Wilkerson and unknown intercessors. However, the lesson that pierced my heart, creating a wound from which I hope never to recover was this: Jesus wants to share things with even His weakest friends, like me. When I lose my place of friendship with God, He misses the friendship and solidarity I could have offered Him. My absence actually affects God's heart.

Consider how God shared His heart with His friends in times when He was releasing judgment upon Israel. Even in the moment of judgment, God was weeping and looking for those to whom He could reveal His deepest motives and plans. He wept with Jeremiah until their tears were so mingled you could not tell where God's tears ended and Jeremiah's began. (See Jeremiah 9:1–2, 17–18.)

In Jeremiah 9, the fierce judgment that was about to be released would decimate Israel, and there would be nothing left standing. Because He wants His resting place to be in man, in the hour of judgment God describes Himself as searching for a place to stay since His people are no longer His home. (See Jeremiah 2:2–3, 31–32.) He too is devastated and shares in all the grief His judgments create.

Where did I go wrong on September 11 to miss out on the friendship we know God seeks in times of judgment? I knew what kinds of things I wanted to hear from Jesus. Did I really want to hear something from God that would become a crushing burden? Did I really want to be weeping over a pending judgment when the rest of the body of Christ was dancing in celebration, oblivious to what was about to happen?

Yet the question still haunts me: What do I want Him to say about me on that day? "Good job with your gift, Shelley," or, "She was My friend! She wept with Me! She carried My heart no matter what it cost her." I came to realize I was not where I thought I was in my friendship with God because, quite frankly, I didn't want to weep with the Lord. I just wanted to hear the word, deliver it, and move on.

I also realized that the desire to grow in my gifts and service to the body of Christ had become a distraction to me. I wanted to execute spiritual gifts, but I was neglecting the real point of knowing God, which is intimate friendship with Jesus. There are many types of prophetic gifts. Some people hear; others see, feel, or know. But the most gifted "seer" can miss out on friendship with God as much as the person who has never seen a vision. God is looking at the heart!

We can easily get confused about God's purpose for the gift of prophecy. The apostle Paul says we should eagerly desire this gift (1 Cor. 14:1), but the reason for our desire is not so we can become part of a group of super prophets who rank spiritual gifts on different levels, rather it is because Jesus Christ is hungry for friends.

Gifts Do Not Equal Intimacy

A painful truth was etched on my heart through the events of September 11, and I would never again assume that spiritual gifts equal friendship with God. I desire an intimacy much deeper than what I can experience by executing a spiritual gift. That desire is in God's heart also. It is called friendship.

Some spiritual gifts can be incredible. For seers, it often seems as if a screen drops down and they see what God is revealing like a movie. Yet as amazing as it can be to receive this kind of revelation, that is not an indication of friendship with God! It is in no way proof of how close a person is to God's heart. It doesn't mean the God-man can pour out His soul to you. And it doesn't mean you're willing to allow yourself to grieve with Him. The most painful thing for me was when the Lord impressed this on my heart:

> Shelley, you still refuse to be affected by My emotions, and that is why I couldn't talk to you about the things that are really on My heart! You want to hear enough to feel like you are saying yes to the call. You even feel like you are a few steps ahead because you are actually in a house of prayer and in a setting where you can have deep study of the Word, including some aspects of God as Judge. You even know a little bit biblically about the reality of judgments that break forth and prepare the earth for My Son's return. You have actually said yes to my wisdom in the Book of Revelation, but Shelley, I don't own your emotions, and I am an emotional Being. It is about My heart. It is not about information; it is not about details. The details don't come unless you are ready to receive My heart and be undone by it.

I was devastated! Again, I don't want to suggest that I should know about every single event that will ever happen, but I knew in my spirit that Jesus wanted to talk to me about September 11 and could not. Why? Because I didn't want to cry. I didn't want to break out in mourning and have everyone around me think I was completely off my rocker. I was concerned about how I would be viewed even at the

International House of Prayer in a community of radical intercessors.

In John 17:24, Jesus says, "Father, I desire that they also whom you gave Me may be *with me where I am*" (emphasis added). Consider this in light of Proverbs 17:17: "A friend loves at all times." What happens when Jesus is in the garden weeping as He did in Matthew 26, and this time He is not getting ready to drink the cup of wrath? This time He already drank it and is preparing to pour it out. Who will weep with Him as He prepares for the greatest hour of judgment the earth has ever seen?

In Revelation 5, the Father hands Jesus the scroll containing His plan for how humanity will be judged. The Lamb who was slain is the only One worthy to bring forth God's righteous judgments. Jesus already drank the cup of wrath. Now He holds the same cup in His hand ready to pour it out, and He is weeping again. What happens when He asks for you? What happens when He says, "Father, I desire this one and that one, that they may be with Me where I am"?

It doesn't matter what your calling is, what your gift mix is, or how the Lord has called you to function within the body of Christ. I can assure you of this: Jesus is hungry for nearness with you. That is His goal. And that is the true spirit of prophecy. It is an answer to the hunger in God's heart. Prophecy is not primarily about getting the word right for this or that person. It is mostly about whether I was listening on the night when Jesus wanted to share His tears or His joy with me.

We are about to enter an unprecedented revival, the likes

of which we have never seen before. I am telling you, seeing God heal Crohn's disease, as He did in my life, will be small compared to what I believe we will see in our day. And this is just the beginning of the beginning.

Intercessors from across the nations are rising up and crying out for an unprecedented move of God, and they will be answered. The lame will walk, the blind will see, signs and wonders will be released, and we will rejoice before King Jesus. And He will be looking for people who will rejoice with Him. Even this revival will bring offense to some believers, who will say, "Why were these healed and those were not?" and, "Why did He heal through that person who was so broken and not through that minister who seemed to have everything together?"

If we think powerful demonstrations of healing and revival will not lead to offense in the hearts of many Christians, we are very poor students of church history. Yet it will not only be the revival that offends. An unprecedented judgment also is going to be released upon the earth before the Lord returns, and the United States is not immune to the dealings of God.

Many Christians did not see September 11 as a judgment from God, but what are we to think? Was God sleeping that day? Did He have His eye on another nation and accidentally allow those planes to become bombs on US soil? Nationalistic pride blinded Israel from recognizing God's judgments upon them, and America is in great danger of making the same mistake. There is no American flag waving before God's throne. He is not an American. He must be true to Himself and judge our nation based on His laws and His kingdom, not on our American dream.

Some Christians dismissed the idea that September 11 was a judgment from God because it was executed by an obviously demonized man, Osama bin Laden. Yet almost all of the judgments God unleashed on the nation of Israel were released through evil regimes. God used wicked rulers and nations to execute His judgments upon other nations; then He inevitably judged the evil nation because it went further than God intended.

God shakes nations and challenges their security so that they might grope for Him. Bin Laden's terrorist network, al Qaeda, is not America's biggest problem; Jesus is. The United States will surely face God's fierce storm if we remove the threat of al Qaeda but do not turn in repentance to God. He will break out with wave after wave of His righteous judgment if the church remains asleep in her bed of comfort while this nation rebels against God's laws by oppressing the poor, killing the unborn, and exporting pornography and other immorality across the earth.

All for Love

As the Judge, Jesus longs for us to weep with Him. As our Bridegroom, He desires that we love and adore Him for who He is. Jesus the King is looking for those who will stand up and celebrate with Him. He wants His church to rejoice in His healing and delivering power.

Some Christians are ready for these two faces of Jesus. They are ready to run, jump, release signs and wonders, pray for the sick, and all those things, but they are reluctant to get up when the Judge comes knocking in the middle of the night. I know there are many details; there are so many things to hash out in this understanding of the Judge, but I have clarity about one thing: the Judge is a Bridegroom, and everything He does, He does in love for love.

I have fallen in love with the Judge. I have come to understand that the right way to approach the Judge is through hunger and desire for justice and righteousness. True and righteous judgments come upon the earth so the nations can learn righteousness (Isa. 26:9). Seeing God's judgments break forth in the earth shows us God's nature, from His commitment to righteousness to His hatred for sin. Our hearts should rejoice in the fact that God hates sin and is committed to challenging it through temporal shakings. Praise God that He hates what has caused the world so much destruction! How has sin affected you? How did it affect your upbringing or your past relationships?

Aren't you glad God is serious about ending sin? In this culture of relativism and moral ambiguity, I am convinced that there is a cry in the hearts of this generation that says, "I need a Judge! Who will fight for me? Who will end the devastation of sin? Who will judge and discipline the nations with righteousness?" If we would quiet our lives and listen, we would hear the deepest part of our hearts crying out as King David did when he said, "My soul breaks with longing for Your judgments at all times" (Ps. 119:20). We long for justice to break out.

Mercy in Judgment

Jesus also wants us to weep with Him over the nations. God does not separate His mind from His emotions as we humans do. We can choose something with our minds because it is wise but not because it affects our emotions. On the other hand, we can choose something based on an emotional response even though it may not be the wisest thing to do. Jesus's wisdom and emotions combine in His heart perfectly with no contradiction. When He executes His judgment, He weeps sometimes and roars at other times. He is emotional, and His heart can be turned.

It is true. In the hour of judgment, God can actually be turned! Why did the Lord tell Jeremiah in essence, "Don't even talk to Me about this because I need to do this"? (See Jeremiah 14:11.) I believe it was because He was warning His friend not to persuade Him to relent. Abraham and Moses also had this level of friendship with God. The Lord would have wiped out His chosen nation, but we read in the Psalms, "Therefore He said that He would destroy them, had not Moses His chosen one stood before Him in the breach, to turn away His wrath, lest He destroy them" (Ps. 106:23).

We also see signs of God's willingness to relent in Joel. The prophet says, "Rend your heart, and not your garments; return to the Lord your God, for He is gracious and merciful, slow to anger, and of great kindness; and He relents from doing harm. Who knows if He will turn and relent, and leave a blessing behind Him—a grain offering and a drink offering for the Lord your God?" (Joel 2:13–14).

I believe with all my being that God is pouring the spirit of prophecy out in this hour (see Joel 2) and is raising up friends of the Judge, who weep with Him and cry out for His mercy, yet set their hearts to love Him at all times. Friendship with the Judge is not optional in this hour of human history. This is part of who He is. In fact, He has stained all of His robes with this specific role of judgment (Isa. 63:3).

I use this made-up analogy, which breaks down on some levels but still gets the job done, so bear with me. Imagine a woman is engaged to a man, and he is a professional tennis player who is getting ready to play at Wimbledon. How ridiculous would it be for her to say, "Well, we are engaged. I am in love with you, but I don't really like that whole tennis thing. I know you are getting ready for Wimbledon. You have been training for it and all, but I don't really want to see you play or to hear much about it. It's nothing personal; I just don't like tennis. I don't understand the scoring process, and it's just not my sport. I love you, though! I can't wait to be married."

It's clear that this would never do. No woman in her right mind would take this posture with the man she loves, and no man in his right mind would stand for this. What about Jesus the Judge? His arm has been fully extended into His activities as righteous Judge, and throughout the Book of Revelation is the promise that He will have an agreeing church. We will know by the Spirit of the Lord, an ardent study of the Scriptures, and our relationship with the Bridegroom when we are to rise up and say, "Turn. Relent, Lord. Mercy," and when we must weep with Him while saying, "True and righteous are Your judgments."

Jeremiah 23:20 says, "In the latter days you will understand it [judgment] perfectly." But the question is, will we take this promise, search out God's heart as Judge, and love Him in the midst of His fierce judgment? Will we love this part of who He is? The Scripture declares that the church will be proudly singing of God's activity as Judge, not only now but also in the age to come.

A professional tennis player headed for Wimbledon has been training his whole life in anticipation of the moment when he can truly display his strength. Jesus also has been preparing for a day when He will show off His strength. It is the day of vengeance that is in His heart when He takes His stand for righteousness once and for all. (See Isaiah 63:4.) He is preparing to demonstrate His power to the nations. Wouldn't we want to love and celebrate Him in that?

There is no way to say, "Well, I want the testimony of Jesus, but only this part and that part!" It is like saying, "I am married to this man, but the Wimbledon thing...it may be a huge activity that he is now committing his strength to, but, you know, I don't really get it, and I don't want to take the time to understand the sport and celebrate as the glory of my husband is put on display. I think I will just stay home."

I know the analogy breaks down in several ways, but perhaps it can still be helpful in underlining an important principle. We cannot ask Jesus to be less than who He is, nor can we choose to only love some of His attributes and discard others. Perhaps it is this forgotten face of Jesus as Judge that is the very face of God we need most. I believe with all of my heart that it is.

Will You Weep With Him?

Jesus is looking for friends. God's friends won't have a critical spirit; they will go around weeping and trembling in holy fascination of the righteous Judge. They will be filled with joy as their hearts embrace the fact that God has healed their wounds. They understand that to be a Bridegroom is to be a Judge, and to be Judge is to be a Bridegroom. There is a grace for us to step into intimacy with God and meet Jesus where He is. I want my life to reflect Jesus's prayer, "Father, I desire that they would be with Me where I am." (See John 17:24.)

If He is treading the winepress, you will find me loving Him there. If He is weeping in the garden, that is where I will be. If He is rejoicing and going out into the harvest to bring in the lost, I will be running with Him on the mountaintops. As He sings His love song over His people, I will sing with Him. I will contribute to that song. He is hungry for me, and I am hungry for Him. Somehow in the depths of God's being He is hungry for friends. How can this be?

In Matthew 26 Jesus displays His deep desire for friends who will weep with Him. When Jesus went to the Garden of Gethsemane to weep over the difficult task before Him, He not only called these three disciples to go with Him, but He also asked three times if they would watch and wait with Him. My heart's desire is that when Jesus knocks on our hearts and asks us to weep with Him in the garden, you and I will be there.

It's a mystery that God even desires friendship with human beings, but He really wanted those disciples to share His tears. He desires that you also would share His tears in this hour. He is not asking for might. He is not asking for perfection. He didn't say, "Father, I desire that they execute spiritual gifts with 100 percent accuracy, never missing the mark." No, Jesus told His Father that the prayer of His heart was that you and I would be with Him where He is and that we would love Him (John 17:24). By the power of the Holy Spirit, we can do that! We can weep with Him and hear His heart by His grace.

When you hear troubling news reports, do you ask Jesus how He feels about it? Make it a habit. When you're reading the newspaper or watching the TV news, take a moment to ask Him how He feels. You are missing out if you don't. He is longing to pour out His heart to you, and regardless of your level of education, you have what He needs: tears and a heart that loves Him.

You don't need money, fame, or success to be a friend of God. You need time—time to move away from life's distractions in order to get quiet before God. The most important thing you'll need is the willingness to take your own escort of pain and meet Him in that place of intimacy. I found out something when I responded to His knock on the painful places in my heart, those areas where I was already weeping, where I was already in my own lament, where I already had my own pain. Jesus was already there. I don't know if they were His tears or mine because somewhere along the way, I exchanged my burdens for His.

I have so much more to understand about this friendship. Sometimes I wake up in the middle of the night, and I can feel the presence of the Lord and His lament about an event in the nations or a friend who is struggling, and I take some time just to listen to His heart. Out of those experiences of hearing God's heart and responding to His request that I weep with Him, I wrote this song, "Weep With Me."

> When I hear You call in the night
> It sounds like a friend
> Longing just to rest for a while
>
> Jesus, lay down Your weary head and weep with me
> Jesus, lay down Your weary head and weep with me
> Jesus, lay down Your weary head and weep with me
>
> One dark night I found the garden where the
>   God-Man weeps alone
> Mixing tears with His judgments I could hear Him
>   long for a home
> And here to answer my heart's longing was a treasure
>
> All my own
> Since I found Him in the garden
> He will never weep alone
>
> Let my tears be Your tears
> Let my heart be Your home
> Come, let me comfort You
> You will not weep alone.

I am so hungry for Jesus to have friends I cannot take it. I am filled with desire. I don't care who hears Him, when, where, or how—I just want Him to be heard! Jesus has things to say. He has feelings for you to feel, and He has a longing in His heart for you to be near to Him! You think your brokenness can compete with the Son of God's prayers that you would be with Him where He is? Your weakness is nothing in comparison to the desire that burns in God's heart to be known. He desires to be known so much that He came to us where we are and became a man forever.

He said, *"Father, I desire... Father, I am longing..."*

He is looking for friends, and His eyes are set upon you. He is not looking for the mighty. He is looking for weak people like you and me who want to be friends of the Judge and will carry His heart to a hurting world.

NOTES

CHAPTER 3
SEEING PAIN THROUGH A NEW LENS

1. C. S. Lewis, *The Problem of Pain* (New York: HarperOne, 2001).

2. Eric Sammons, "The Quotable St. Teresa of Avila," The Divine Life, October 15, 2009, http://ericsammons.com/blog/2009/10/15/the-quotable-st-teresa-of-avila/ (accessed March 20, 2011).